Management
and
Organizational
Development

McGRAW-HILL SERIES IN MANAGEMENT

KEITH DAVIS, Consulting Editor

Management and Organizational Development

The Path from XA to YB

CHRIS ARGYRIS

Beach Professor of Administrative Sciences
Yale University

McGRAW-HILL BOOK COMPANY

New York   St. Louis   San Francisco   Düsseldorf
Johannesburg   Kuala Lumpur   London   Mexico
Montreal   New Delhi   Panama   Rio de Janeiro
Singapore   Sydney   Toronto

This book was set in Alphatype Astro by University Graphics, and printed on permanent paper and bound by The Book Press. The editors were Dale L. Dutton and Barbara Church. The designer was Naomi Auerbach. Teresa F. Leaden supervised production.

To Leland P. Bradford

Contents

Preface

At the heart of organizational development is the concern for the vitalizing, energizing, actualizing, activating, and renewing of organizations through technical and human resources. Technical development is achieved through areas of marketing, finance, engineering, and manufacturing. Human-resource development concerns people, interpersonal relationships, small groups, intergroups, and organizational norms and values.

The technical resources are interrelated with the human resources. Thus an executive with high self-acceptance and who is a member of an effective management group may tend to create and use financial controls in a more constructive manner than an executive with low self-acceptance who is a member of an ineffective management group. Also a well-designed financial-control system can enhance the opportunities for human cooperation and increase the self-acceptance of individual executives.

This book focuses on the human resources. It asks how a quality of life can be created and maintained within an organization so that the participants

1. Produce valid and useful information especially about their more important problems.

2. Make effective decisions.

3. Generate a high degree of human energy and commitment to their decisions in order to diligently monitor and effectively implement them.

I will begin the exploration by following the advice of Douglas McGregor who suggested that management in any organization examine carefully the fundamental assumptions it makes about human beings, that is, the fundamental theory it holds about the effective management of people. Why examine the fundamental assumptions management holds about people? Because these assumptions tend to act as axioms for much of management policy and practice. If you know the assumptions management makes about the nature of people, it is possible to explain much about the organizational structure, leadership behavior, and control mechanisms that will be used in the organization. You can also predict the probable responses of the people to these crucial aspects of organizations. In a system where there are people with more power and people with less power (as is the case in most organizations), the latter tend to reduce the inequality increasing the negative, unintended, and undesirable effects implicit in the management assumptions. This in turn, reduces the probability that an organization will produce valid information (especially about important organizational issues), reduces decision-making effectiveness, and reduces the overall commitment to the decisions made.

The focus is on people, not because we are unconcerned about organizations but because people create and maintain organizations. Also, it is people who must design, accept, and implement changes that are required to keep the organization in a healthy state.

This brings us to the subtitle of the book. X stands for theory X, A for pattern A. Theory X is the title given by Douglas McGregor to a set of assumptions management has that people cannot be trusted, and prefer to be controlled by, and to be dependent upon, their management for all actions. Pattern A represents the writer's findings on the interpersonal behavior, group dynamics, and organizational norms that tend to be associated with theory X. Theory Y, according to McGregor, is another set of management assumptions that is more consistent with the potentialities of man as described by recent research. For example, it assumes that man can be more of an active contributor to his and to the organization's well-being. Pattern B represents the interpersonal behavior, group dynamics, and organizational norms associated with theory Y.

This book is about three organizations which decided to begin to travel the road from XA toward YB. In doing so, top management realized that both XA and YB were necessary oversimplifications. Life was too complex to be so easily categorized. But the very simplicity of the concepts made experimentation possible.

Two points should be emphasized. First, no one is suggesting that XA is all bad, nor that YB is all good. Indeed, the writer has suggested decision rules specifying some of the conditions under which each structure is probably most effective (Argyris, 1962; 1964). The point of the book, is to focus on the management experimentation in three organizations to go from XA toward YB. Second, theory and behavior may go together, but not necessarily so. We will return to this point later.

The objectives of this book

The book is written for the line executive and for the professional consultant or interventionist in organizational development. The primary message I should like to communicate is that the trip from XA toward YB is not an easy one. And why should it be? As we shall see, most leaders in any type of organization tend to be programmed by their society to value theory X and to behave according to pattern A. They are taught that strong leaders are those who control and manage others. They are cautioned not be become too self-conscious or get too close to people. "In business you've got to be fair and you've got to be firm. But, by jessuz, you've got to be firm." They are admonished not to accept a new idea about management until it has been proven by someone else. They are cautioned not to trust the average worker's motivation. As one executive put it, "5 percent of the people work; 10 percent think they work; and 85 percent would rather die than work."

These beliefs tend to create executives who are eager to manage others, but anxious about managing themselves; who are ready to be hard and cold in getting the job done, but are capable of tears when they are publicly acclaimed for their accomplishments; who resist delegating authority and responsibility, but gladly delegate to others the responsibility of accommodating to their leadership style; who speak of innovation and creativity, but hesitate, and in some cases ridicule, those who strive to experiment with YB.

Moreover the behavioral scientists, as we hope to show, have not generated the systematic theory nor the empirically tested knowledge that would help the line executive and the organizational development professional to be more effective in guiding executives from XA to YB. Because of the paucity of research, the education available to an executive wishing to experiment with YB is less than that available to someone who wants to be a Junior Red Cross lifesaver. The follow-up help available after one goes through the admittedly primitive educational experiences, is scarce, generally not of high quality, and too often undependable. Finally, we consultants who are available differ greatly in our competence, but are remarkably alike in the wide areas of common ignorance about effective organizational change and design.

Consequently, I have become anxious since less unrealistically high expectations are created among key people in our society who are thinking about experimenting with the trip from XA toward YB. False expectations easily lead to unrealistic levels of aspiration, which in turn may lead to frustration, dismay, and discouragement, which in turn could cause some people (those well-established) to bury themselves deeper in tradition, while others (those not so well-established) blow themselves off (while blowing other people up) from their society.

To repeat, one of the primary purposes of the book is to say that the trip, although exciting, fundamental, and essential, is difficult, exhausting, and frustrating. The reader will find no pat answers, no clear-cut, tested guideposts, no simplistic scenarios where the good can be separated from the bad; where no matter how deep the conflict, it is overcome by a dynamic speech or a guilt-producing occurrence; where, in the end, all is well and the good are rewarded. The book is filled, perhaps repetitively so, with struggle, conflict, groping, bewilderment, anger, frustration, and above all the continual amazement and dismay of the participants. You can almost feel them as they ask, "Does it have to be *this* difficult?"; "Is it worth all the inner conflict, tension, and fear?"

Yes, fear is high in the hearts of many of the executives studied, although they may be unwilling to talk about it. One perceptive top executive, when discussing his experiences in groping toward YB, put it as follows, "You know, I thought of the 23d Psalm as I read the manuscript. 'Though I walk through the valley of the shadow of death I will fear no evil.' Boy, it isn't true. You fear all the time."

The second major objective is to provide the professional consultant with suggestions on how to deal with some of these problems or at least how to face them squarely and openly. The hope is that the theory and the documented experiences will help the consultant not only to face but to deal with the problems of going from XA toward YB and to be more effective in giving help to the client and will help the client in asking for and receiving help from the consultant. I also hope that it will stimulate interventionists or consultants to conduct more research on our behavior in order that we can accelerate the speed with which effective theory of and methods in consulting can be developed.

I hope that the book will also be read by undergraduates and graduate students (especially in professional schools). I would like them to see that there *are* executives who are trying hard to raise the quality of organizational life; who continually face resistance, fear, and anger from their peers, subordinates, and if the entire story were told, in some cases, from their families and religious and community leaders who respond in disbelief that imaginative and humanistic experiments can come from business leaders in our society.

My deepest appreciation goes to the top executives of

organizations A, B, and C who not only put up with me, but permitted me and encouraged me to write this book. I should also like to thank my colleagues Edward Lawler III, Roy Lewicki, and Gerrit Wolf for their helpful comments. Mrs. Maryellen Holford was invaluable in typing and editing the manuscript.

The book is dedicated to Doctor Leland P. Bradford. As the director of the NTL Institute of Applied Behavioral Sciences, he helped to bring to life the first network of behavioral scientists and practitioners designed to apply behavioral science knowledge to some of the key human problems of the world. He introduced me to the world of experiential learning and encouraged me in my research and consulting efforts. When the history of applied behavioral science is written, Lee Bradford will be seen as one of the few who worked tirelessly to help the many.

Chris Argyris

Chapter one
Introduction

Three top-management groups in three very different organizations had something in common. Although the top management in each organization was at a different point in its decision making about organizational development, they were all struggling to design more effective organizations. They wanted to make their organizations healthier and to raise the quality of life in them.

Organization A had recently begun to think about organizational development. The starting point of interest was the care and feeding of their younger managers. They wanted to be able to identify the most competent managers early. More important, they wanted to think more systematically about their careers so that the younger men could be exposed to job experiences that would keep them involved, continuously challenged, and constantly learning. The top management believed that if they could create such conditions the organization and the younger executives, as human beings, would gain. Existing research supports their beliefs (Dunnette, Arvey, and Banas, 1970; Berlew and Hall, 1966; and Schein, 1964).

The difficulties involved in creating a genuine organizational-development activity hit the top-management group when the writer was able to help them to see that organizational development would have to begin with them; that it implied a commitment to a philosophy of management that was paradoxically as popular as motherhood and as painful to implement as anything that they had ever tried. When confronted with the possibility that their behavior may have to change, because they were (unknowingly) inhibiting more individual growth than possibly any other set of factors, they responded by becoming cynical about changing human behavior, by expressing fears that they might become too worried about people, which would result in soft management.

In this response, we find one of the most challenging problems in organizational development. On the one hand, there is a genuine interest in human beings. On the other hand, there are strong fears about the consequences of human growth and a deep pessimism about human beings changing their behavior.

Haire, Ghiselli, and Porter (1963) have reported these apparently contradictory views about man and management in a worldwide study. Argyris (1969) has found it to exist, in addition to business executives, in secondary school teachers; professors of physical science, humanities, social sciences; architects; accountants; engineers; trade union leaders; college students; indeed, everyone so far studied. Why do people hold such humanistically optimistic and deeply cynical and gloomy views about human nature?

This is a crucial problem in all organizational development. As we shall see, in all three organizations it remained a key issue, an issue that could smother change or provide it with an impetus that was to surprise even the executives themselves.

The top management in organization B held similar values about the development of young talent. However, their initial stimulus for organizational development came from the realization that their paternalistic philosophy of the past supplied little momentum for growth in the future. They had developed plans for growth, and they now realized that they had not developed the attitudes and skills within management to take initiative, make decisions, and take risks.

The top management had been evolving an organizational-development activity for nearly two years when the writer became a consultant to them. About half of the top group had very meaningful experiences at executive laboratories (primarily given by NTL Institute of Behavioral Science). All of them in this subgroup had been responsible for a "strong" leadership during the past several decades. They now realized, through an organizational analysis, that such leadership had serious unintended consequences. Apparently the only thing that remained strong, under strong leadership, were the executives with the most power who could "get things done" and who rarely received feedback about the instantaneous deterioration and the creeping infection that was leisurely polluting the system they wanted to make dynamic and alive.

The other half of the membership of the top-management group were new additions. They had not attended laboratories, and many of them had serious questions about the value of such experiences and about the philosophy of management implicit in organizational development. Like the top management in organization A, they all valued human growth in the abstract and during dinner conversations, especially with subordinates they wished to keep. However, unlike organization A, those top executives who were committed to organizational development were committed to it emotionally and intellectually. They wanted to see human beings develop themselves because they believed it to be in their organization's interest *and* because they valued human growth. They were ready to explore the creation of conditions for human growth, even if the individual to be involved preferred to remain in a dependent, submissive posture. Although they were not ambivalent about the value of human growth, they did not intend (indeed they knew it would be folly to attempt) to order it or require it.

Their genuine commitment to organizational development ran smack into the genuine disbelief of such activities by the other members of their own top-management team. This resulted in two subgroups. The intergroup rivalries and hostilities created by the disagreement became the context within which issues of human growth, the feasibility of human change, the practicality and advisability of trust, and the fear of going soft were examined and worked through.

How difficult these issues are to identify, work through, and translate into managerial policy that works! If the reader has any doubts, they may be dispelled when he learns that the top management of organization C were also dealing with these issues after five years of serious organizational effort. During that time the entire top management had attended (what they reported to be) meaningful and successful experiential laboratories; the president and the top officers had given approval to commit funds to design and execute a large organizational-development program; and an excellent professional staff had been assembled to help the organization in its development.

The study of organization C will also help us to see that an important barrier to progress is the primitive state of the field of organizational development. Time and time again the top executives sought some maps, guidelines to help them in redesigning the organization. In most cases they were frustrated because they were simply not available. The professionals in organizational development seemed to be more at home in designing and executing T-groups. They floundered in the design of new organizational structures and administrative controls. Unless research in these areas is greatly increased, what few gains that have been made in organizational development may be eradicated. Effective interpersonal relationships are a necessary but not a sufficient condition for organizational growth.

The intellectual origins of organizational development

In his monograph, Bennis (1969) has described the conditions which created the need for organizational development. They are rapid and unexpected change, organizational growth (in size), increasing diversity, and change in managerial behavior. These conditions help us to understand the problems that organizational development confronts in actual ongoing systems.

There is a need to explore, even briefly, the intellectual origins of organizational development. In addition to helping us see how the concept evolved, history may help us to understand more clearly some of the field's present inconsistencies and ineffectiveness. Also it is hoped that it can shed light on some of the future directions research and practice may need to take.

Mayo (1933) and Roethlesberger and Dickson (1949) provided one of the early beginning points. The now famous "Hawthorne effect" established that people will work hard and put up with difficult working conditions if they feel that the objective is worth doing. People apparently want to be involved in and to participate in meaningful activities. Lewin (1951) and his students, who came from a different intellectual background, also produced research to show that participation may lead to more productivity, greater commitment, and greater personal satisfaction. Lewin and his students went further to show that participation is worthwhile and useful because people have important contributions to make. Indeed, they questioned the genuineness of participation if the individuals were not making significant contributions.

What inhibits participation? Directive, authoritarian leaders do (Lewin, 1951) who are more production-centered than people-centered (Likert, 1961); whose initiation of action is significantly greater than their subordinates' (Whyte, 1961); who focus on initiating structure at the expense of concern for people (Fleishman, 1961); who create more dependence and submissiveness on the part of their subordinates (McGregor, 1944).

Argyris (1957) added the organizational structure (including technology), administrative controls, and pseudo-human relations programs to causes of dependence and inhibitors of participation. He hypothesized that the frustrated people would tend to be those who aspired toward "maturity" or "psychological success" and were not permitted by their jobs or those who aspired toward "immaturity" and "psychological failure." He suggested that in real life, the overwhelming number of the cases would be in the former condition.

He also suggested that if people were frustrated in organizations, they would tend to react by such activities as absenteeism, turnover, emphasis on material rewards, apathy, indifference, goldbricking, and psychological withdrawal, as well as the creation of trade unions.

McGregor, who had a keen insight into top-management thinking, wrote a book expressly to reach this audience, to inform them of the behavioral science research about *The Human Side of Enterprise*. He based his analysis on the assertion that management had created a work world that had in it an implicit theory about the nature of man. By "theory," McGregor meant that managers were operating from a systematic, interrelated (but implicit) set of generalizations that significantly influenced their behavior. He called it "theory X." Its major assumptions were:

1. The average human being has an inherent dislike of work and will avoid it if he can.

2. Because of this human characteristic of dislike of work, most people must be coerced, controlled, directed, threatened with punishment to get them to put forth adequate effort toward the achievement of organizational objectives.

3. The average human being prefers to be directed, wishes to avoid responsibility, has relatively little ambition, wants security above all (McGregor, 1960, pp. 3–31).

There were, according to McGregor, two difficulties with these assumptions. First, they did not fit the picture of human nature that social scientists were developing. Second, they pervaded management policy and practice and

raised havoc with human motivation, growth, and commitment to productivity.

Not so, replied some sociologists. The theory X assumption may not jibe with those that some behavioral scientists were evolving, but that did not make much difference
for several reasons. First, the idea that people sought self-
realization (Maslow, 1954) in the form of not being dependent and submissive (Argyris, 1954) was a middle-
class concept that did not fit the reality of working-class
attitudes (Strauss, 1963). Second, workers no longer considered work as a central life interest (Dubin, 1963; Goldthorpe et al., 1968). Therefore, third, happiness and satisfaction at work were no longer relevant (Strauss, 1963).

The difficulty with the first position is that it ignores
the ample evidence to the contrary. As the studies summarized by Argyris show, workers do report needs to use
their abilities and to have control over their work (Argyris,
1964, pp. 78–86). Recently Tannenbaum (1968) published
a review of empirical research on organizational control in
200 organizational units in America. He reports that employees, at all levels, seek more control over their work
world which, if achieved, would place them in situations
where they would be less dependent and submissive. It
is at the level of the *rank and file* where the greatest gap
is reported between the actual control the workers have
and the amount they wished they had. Zupanov and Tannenbaum (1968) report similar results for subjects in
Yugoslavia. Also, workers whose jobs are enlarged initially find work more difficult but eventually express
gratitude for being able to work at more meaningful jobs
(Argyris, 1970). Here are examples of workers changing
their attitudes *without* changing their social class.

Goldthorpe et al. (1968) present voluminous evidence

in their own work that employees may no longer seek self-realization at work because it is not available in the jobs they are asked to perform. There is little doubt, however, if one reads the employee quotation included, that they would value such work.

For example:

The employees who were most satisfied were "setters" because of opportunity (Goldthorpe et al., 1968)

To use their skills:	"Being a setter draws more skill out of you. There's nothing to being an operator. [As a setter] you have to use your brains more. . . ." (p. 13)
To control own work:	"You're left alone—there's only myself on the job. You go along nicely on your own." (p. 13)
To use own initiative:	"I've more opportunity to work on my own initiative and figure things out for myself." (p. 13)
To have variety:	"There's nothing monotonous about it. Most machining is cut up so much that it's all repetition." (p. 13)

The employees who were least satisfied were assemblers whose jobs lacked these characteristics (pp. 14–17).

It is probably true that many workers may have de-emphasized the importance of work and taken on what Goldthorpe et al. (1968) and Dubin (1963) call an "instrumental view." Maurer (1969) citing Argyris (1957) shows that the latter predicted that this could become one way for the affluent worker to adapt.

Finally, the inconsistency in the position taken by Strauss (1963) that workers do not seek happiness or satisfaction is shown by his own argument when he invokes happiness as the reason that workers do not seek self-expression while at work!

To summarize to date: Management may have based the makeup of the organizational world on incorrect assumptions about human nature. Due to their power to make self-fulfilling prophecies, they may have created a world in which the "incorrect" assumptions actually become workable. Unfortunately, the cost for making incorrect assumptions may be uncommitted, uninvolved, lower-level employees who increasingly withdraw their concern for organizational health.

In addition to making incorrect assumptions about human nature, management may have also been making incorrect assumptions about effective interpersonal relationships (Argyris, 1966). Indeed, more recent research suggests these incorrect assumptions may be held by the population in general. They may have become learned through the normal processes of acculturation and education (Argyris, 1969).

Focusing on managers and executives, for the purposes of this account, it has been found that they may be "programmed" or hold three values (internalized commands) about effective human relationships. They are:

1. The significant human relationships are the ones which have to do with achieving the organization's objective.

2. People are most effective when they are rational. They are least effective when they express feelings and emotions.

3. Human relationships are most effectively influenced through unilateral direction, coercion, and control, as

well as rewards and penalties that sanction all three values.

What impact do these values have upon decision making, upon intergroup relations, upon organizational health, and upon executive relationships?

To date, the results of twenty-eight groups in fifteen different organizations, participating in 163 different meetings have been published. These meetings were observed, tape-recorded, analyzed, and scored by a set of categories developed by the writer. The methods used are discussed in slightly more detail because they were also used in studying the top management of organizations A, B, and C.

The observational categories used in this research are graphically summarized in Table 1. The categories above the zero line are hypothesized to facilitate interpersonal

TABLE 1 *Categories of Behavior*

Level I		Level II
Individual	Interpersonal	Norms
Experimenting *i* *f*	Helping others to *i* experiment *f*	Trust *i* *f*
Openness *i* *f*	Helping others to be *i* open *f*	Concern *i* *f*
Owning *i* *f*	Helping others to *i* own *f*	Individuality *i* *f*
———————— Zero line ————————		
Not owning *i* *f*	Not helping others to *i* own *f*	Conformity *i* *f*
Not open *i* *f*	Not helping others to *i* be open *f*	Antagonism *i* *f*
Rejecting ex- *i* perimenting *f*	Not helping others to *i* experiment *f*	Mistrust *i* *f*

relationships, those below the line to inhibit interpersonal relationships. Each category has an idea (*i*) and a feeling (*f*) component. The categories positioned closest to the zero line are the easiest to perform, and those farthest away are the most difficult. For example, it is easier to own up to one's ideas or feelings (to express one's views and feelings) than it is to experiment with ideas or feelings (to discuss those ideas or feelings that, if wrong, would jeopardize one's self-acceptance). There are two levels of analyses. Level I represents the individual and interpersonal. Level II represents norms of the group. Every unit of behavior is scored on both levels. For example:

Sample statement		*Would be scored as*
1. I believe that we should reject the idea, even though we are told not to.	own *i*	individuality *i*
2. I feel tense.	own *f*	individuality *f*
3. Would you please tell me more about your theory?	open *i*	concern *i*
4. This is not easy for me to talk about. I feel as if my whole life has been a shambles. I feel frightened and bewildered.	experimenting *f*	trust *f*

Some findings about the "typical" interpersonal world (pattern A)

A total of 45,802 units of behavior were recorded in 163 different meetings. Some of the relevant findings are:

1. Only six categories (of the thirty-six available) were frequently observed. The categories used most frequently (i.e., they accounted for at least 75 percent of the scores

in a given meeting) were (in order of frequency observed) own *i*, concern *i*, conform *i*. Categories that accounted for about 20 percent of the scores were open *i*, individuality *i*, and antagonism *i*. (The "*i*" means the behavior was observed to be intellective and not an expression of feelings.) The remaining 5 percent were spread variously over the other categories.

2. Rarely (and in most sessions, never) were individuals in groups observed expressing feelings, being open to feelings, experimenting with ideas or feelings. Rarely observed were the norms of concern, individuality, and trust related to feelings; the norm of trust related to ideas; and the norm of mistrust related to ideas or feelings.

3. Rarely observed were individuals in groups helping each other own up to, be open toward, and experiment with ideas or feelings. We will call this pattern of variables "pattern A."

From these data one may infer that the interpersonal world of the individuals in the groups studied is one in which individuals tended to express their ideas in such a way that they supported the norms of concern for, or conformity to, ideas. They were significantly less open to ideas and expressed (slightly less so) their ideas in such a way that supported the norms of individuality or antagonism.

Individuals did not, nor did group norms, support their owning up to their feelings, being open to their own and others' feelings. There was almost no experimenting with ideas and feelings and also no trust existing in the groups. Rarely did individuals help others to own up to, be open with, and experiment with ideas and feelings. People rarely said what they believed about the important issues if they perceived them to be potentially threatening to any member. They preferred to be "diplomatic," "careful," "not make waves." Under these conditions, valid information about *unimportant* issues (task or interpersonal) was easy to obtain. It was very difficult to obtain valid information regarding *important* issues (task or interpersonal). It was very difficult to problem solve effectively about these important issues, since people tended to cover up important information. Also, individuals rarely received valid information about threatening issues. For example, in a study of 199 important influence attempts (among a group of twenty executives, over a period of a year), 134 failed and 65 succeeded. In only two cases was honest feedback given about the failures. In all other cases the individual attempting to have the influence was assured that he had succeeded when, in fact, he had not. Of successes, 54 represented influence attempts made by the president. The observers reported that the influence attempts succeeded in that the president got across the message that he wanted. However, in 48 cases the subordinates felt hostile toward him. None of them communicated these feelings to the president.

The game of telling people what they "should" hear and the consequent lack of valid information understandably led individuals to be blind about their impact upon others. However, they were able to be accurate (in an interview) about the impact others had on them (if they felt they could trust the researcher).

The answer, put simply, is that the values tend to create executive relationships with more mistrust than trust, closedness than openness, conformity than individuality, emphasis on stability than risk taking. These conditions act to decrease the effectiveness of decision making and intergroup relations, and lower the organization's health (Argyris, 1968).

Two recent tragic examples are the apparent massacres

by American troops in Vietnam and the near-resignations of key Johnson aides over the war. Concerning the former, the *New York Times* reports that "the Army's secret report on the Songmy incident concluded that each successive level of command received a more watered-down account of what had actually occurred in the village" (*New York Times*, 1970). As to the latter, Hoopes describes the agony of several top-level subordinates who did not agree with the President but did not believe they could communicate their true feelings upward and be heard (Hoopes, 1969).

If we integrate the previous findings with these, we come to two major conclusions:

1. In the social universe, where presumably there is no mandatory state of entropy, man can claim the dubious distinction of creating organizations that generate entropy, that is, slow but certain processes toward system deterioration.

2. Organizations, as information-processing systems, will tend to produce *invalid* information for the important, risky, threatening issues (where ironically they need valid information badly) and valid information for the unimportant, routine issues.

What can be done to reverse the processes of organizational entropy and ineffective information processing?

McGregor's response to this question was to develop a new theory, which he called "theory Y." The theory asserted certain assumptions about human nature which he felt were congruent with the evolving behavioral science knowledge about man. McGregor also counseled management (1) not to use the theory unless they genuinely meant to behave or design organizations in accordance with its assumptions, (2) that a partial use of theory was more dangerous than a complete but open rejection of it, (3) that change will require much hard work and unfreezing, (4) that they continually test the theory as they went along, so that it took on the qualities of a theory and not an ideology.

The assumptions of theory Y were:

1. The expenditure of physical and mental effort in work is as natural as play or rest.

2. External control and the threat of punishment are not the only means for bringing about effort toward organizational objectives. Man will exercise self-direction and self-control in the service of objectives to which he is committed.

3. Commitment to objectives is a function of the reward associated with their achievement.

4. The average human being learns, under proper conditions, not only to accept but to seek responsibility.

5. The capacity to exercise a relatively high degree of imagination, ingenuity, and creativity in the solution of organizational problems is widely, not narrowly, distributed in the population.

6. Under the conditions of modern industrial life, the intellectual potentialities of the average human being are partially utilized (McGregor, 1960, pp. 42–48).

Such assumptions, according to McGregor, would lead management to design superior-subordinate relationships where the subordinate had greater influence over the activities involved in his work and greater probability of influencing his superior's actions. Likert (1967) enlarged the scope of change to the entire organization. Likert (1967) and Marrow, Bowers, and Seashore (1967) presented em·

pirical evidence that a participative or System IV management could be more effective. Likert's System IV was based on:

Organizational variables	That required
1. Leadership processes	1. High confidence and trust.
2. Motivational forces	2. Economic rewards based on compensation system developed through genuine participation
3. Communication processes	3. Free and valid flow of information at all levels
4. Interaction-influence processes	4. High degree of mutual confidence and trust
5. Decision making	5. Wide involvement and well integrated through linking processes
6. Control processes	6. Wide responsibility for review and control at all levels (Likert, 1969, pp. 4–10)

Burns and Stalker's (1961) suggestion of organic organization, Bennis's (1959) open system, Litwak's (1961) "human relations system" were congruent with Likert's views. Argyris (1964) attempted to show that these conceptions were congruent with the very nature of the concept of organization, whether at the crystal, cellular, organ, or social group levels. The empirical research was, therefore, focusing on some basic processes of living and nonliving nature. He further proposed that the organization of the future would have different organizational structures for different decisions as well as different managerial controls (Argyris, 1962; 1964).

It was also suggested that the interpersonal competence,

especially of the people in power, would have to be increased if valid information about important issues was to flow. More trust, concern for feelings, and internal commitment; more openness to, and experimenting with, new ideas and feelings *in such a way that others could do the same*, were recommended if valid information was to be produced and internal commitment to decisions generated (Argyris, 1962; 1965). He called the new cluster of behavior "pattern B."

Note that it is not recommended that an individual be completely open, or show complete trust. The key is for A, for example, to be open to the extent that it also permits B to be open. Openness, therefore, is not something in an individual. True openness or trust exists only in interpersonal relationships. One asks, therefore, how open the relationship is between A and B; not how open A or B is (Argyris, 1962). This implies that A adjusts his degree of openness to how he believes he will be heard most accurately and completely by B *and* what will help B express himself most accurately and completely. If A believes that B is not open to as much relevant information as A has, then A can explore the issue with B as to how to widen the channels of communication. To say what you believe is to be honest; to say what you believe in such a way that the other can do the same is to be authentic (Argyris, 1962).

It should be emphasized that although XA and YB are *usually* associated with each other in everyday life, they do not have to be. Under certain conditions pattern A could go with theory Y or pattern B with theory X. An example of the first case is presented in Chapter 3. The consultant was being openly and frequently condemned and his views systematically distorted by several clients. After several attempts to change the relationship through pattern B behavior failed, he finally said in effect, "Now hear this,

I'm not going to continue to let you get away with what you're doing." This intervention was necessary to "break through" the defenses of the client. It was done with the assumption that the client could be trusted to wish to grow, to be responsible for his behavior, to learn.

An example of pattern B behavior being associated with theory X is the case illustrated by the question, "Isn't it possible for someone to become more trusting, more open, show more concern, and use it to continue being manipulative?" The answer is "yes," but only for a while *if* the other members feel free to be confronting. A manipulator in theory Y clothing soon betrays himself. This key issue of a time limit applies to both cases. If the consultant continues to badger the client (in the first case), then one could question his apparent commitment to theory Y.

These cases illustrate the point, until recently under-emphasized in the literature. Theories are a set of concepts and assumptions that suggest certain behavior under given conditions. When McGregor first discussed these theories, he focused almost exclusively on the conditions where X would go with pattern A and Y with pattern B because, he believed, these were the two conditions that existed most frequently and strongly, a belief which the writer shares. However, a theory becomes complete when it also accounts for the less frequent conditions. This is why the emphasis in recent years has been on different styles of leadership or structure for different conditions, e.g., reality-centered (Argyris, 1957), culture-centered (Likert, 1967), and contingency theory (Fiedler, 1967).

If we examine these historical events we will find several basic trends:

1. A sense of importance and a feeling of participation identified in the early Hawthorne studies were enlarged to give the employee genuine influence and power to

plan significantly his work world. It is interesting to note that Blumberg (1966), in a reexamination of some of the original Hawthorne data, suggested it was this type of participation that produced the results in relay room and not the fact that the employees were part of an experiment.

2. Changes in leadership style were expanded to changes in the entire organization (its structure, control systems, personnel policies, etc.).

3. Focus on satisfaction and morale was enlarged to include trust, self-responsibility, and internal commitment.

4. The focus on the maintenance of the internal system was enlarged to include the organization's adaptation or coping with the external world (Burns and Stalker, 1961; Lawrence and Lorsch, 1967; Schein, 1965).

When connecting the environment with the organization Burns and Stalker and Lawrence and Lorsch argue that a more mechanistic organization may be appropriate in a benign environment, while the organic may be best suited for a more turbulent environment. This generalization may be oversimplified if the generalization about organizational entropy is valid. If organizational entropy exists, then the organizations will tend to deteriorate and develop what John Gardner has called "dry rot." Eventually their malignancy will spread throughout the entire system. Workers may soon begin to produce poorly. This, in turn, places them in a turbulent environment—indeed Gardner has suggested that our entire society could be destroyed if our institutions do not change (Gardner, 1968). In short, given the predisposition toward organizational entropy, an organization always has an internal turbulent state, no matter what the state of the external environment; the danger is to think that there are benign states.

The top management of organizations A, B, and C, although managing different kinds of organizations, held in common the belief that there was never a benign environment, that "benign neglect" was the source of "hidden death."

A theoretical framework about intervention

In the section above, I have tried to summarize briefly some major historical trends in research, ending with a few generalizations about present theory and practice regarding organizations.

The other coequal focus is the interventionist or consultant. What is his impact on organizational health and development? Are there consulting strategies that are more effective than others? Unfortunately, the research about intervention is significantly more primitive than that about organizations. The field is so young that its history is just beginning to take form. Consequently it is difficult to identify historical trends and present a coherent picture of present practice.

Recently, the writer outlined a theoretical framework about consulting (Argyris, 1970). I should like to use it as a guide for analyzing consulting and organizational development activities in this book.

Since the theoretical framework is available, only a few comments will be stated in order to familiarize the reader with some of its major ideas.

1. The probability of generating valid information increases (between two or more individuals or groups) when:

(a) Self-acceptance, feelings of essentiality, and valid confirmation of oneself are higher than feelings of low self-acceptance, lack of essentiality, and nonconfirmation or invalid confirmation.

(b) The experience of psychological success is higher than that of psychological failure.

(c) The relevant information is communicated in directly verifiable or observable categories. Information communicated through inferred or indirectly verifiable categories is kept at a minimum; or when the inferred categories are communicated, the raw data from which the inferences were made are also communicated.

This means that whenever possible (i.e., in human relationships, policy statements, directives) evaluative, attributive, and mutually contradictory information should be minimized.

(d) The leadership in groups is assigned according to the abilities of the individuals and in keeping with the needs of the members.

(e) All the members feel internal commitment for the effective management of the group (e.g., keeping it "on target," concern about providing climate for open exchange of views, high trust among members, etc.).

2. The probability of an intervention being effective in helping the clients move toward YB increases as the interventionist adheres to three primary tasks. They are:

(a) Generating and helping the clients to generate valid information that they can understand about their problems.

(b) Creating opportunities for the clients to search effectively for solutions to their problems, to make free choices.

(c) Creating conditions for internal commitment to these choices and apparatus for the continual monitoring of the action taken.

These three primary tasks are hypothesized to be relevant for an intervention of any magnitude. They may also be conceived of as three processes in any intervention, be it a ten-minute discussion, a two-hour task meeting, a T-group, or an extended organizational development program. When viewed as processes, the action implication is that an intervention begins with generating valid information, then moves on to client search and decision, and finally to internal commitment and monitoring.

3. Some of the conditions under which an interventionist probably has to work may be specified *if* we may assume that the present client systems tend toward theory X and pattern A (XA), and (as is the case in organizations A, B, and C) they are interested in moving toward YB philosophy and behavior. The conditions are:

(a) There is a tendency toward an underlying discrepancy between the interventionist's and client's behavior, values, and criteria which each uses to judge effectiveness. Discrepancies tend to exist regarding the causes of problems, the new designs necessary to remedy the situation, and the behavior that is necessary on the part of interventionist and client.

The discrepancy problem may be compounded by a discrepancy the interventionist experiences between his own ideas and his actual behavior.

(b) The discrepancy tends to place the interventionist in a marginal role. He holds membership in two overlapping, but different, worlds.

(c) Clients tend to be more clear about their confusion, frustration, and mistrust of the interventionist than about the order and trust he is attempting to help establish.

(d) The interventionist will tend to receive minimal feedback about his effectiveness, or lack thereof, even though his theory and style require such feedback to keep him as effective as possible.

4. Effectiveness under the conditions above is very difficult. However, one can increase the probability that he

can help the system to generate valid information (e.g., directly observable categories), free choice, and internal commitment by:

(a) Having a relatively high degree of self-awareness and self-acceptance.

(b) Having a high degree of confidence in the validity and the consistency of one's intervention philosophy. (Genuine confidence also tends to lead to the greatest willingness to have the philosophy confronted and tested.)

(c) Perceiving stressful reality accurately.

(d) Valuing the client's attacks and mistrust as necessary for him and as useful points of departure for progress.

(e) Trusting his own experience of reality, especially when the client may insist his experience is distorted. (High trust occurs if the interventionist can subject his experience to confrontation and empirical test.)

(f) Designing growth experiencing in stressful environments.

As the case analysis unfolds, we expect to relate these hypothesized conditions of effectiveness to what actually occurred. When data, hard or soft, of effectiveness are presented, can one also document that one or a combination of the above existed? Was effectiveness found to exist under different conditions? Was failure found to exist under the conditions above?

A note on research methods

The fundamental research assumption being made in this monograph is that important progress can be made in a field by identifying ". . . systematic relationships among diverse phenomena" (Geertz, 1965, pp. 105–107). We asked, if we were to examine three different organizations at three different points in their decision making about organizational development, what would we learn? Are they facing similar or different problems? Why? How are the problems coped with? What implications can be identified for the practice and theory of organizational development?

The research methods used to study these systems were primarily observational and secondarily interview. The focus of analysis was the processes that existed among the relevant units within the client system and between these units and the interventionist. Processes may be studied in a time-series design with quantitative data that can be responsive to the many questions raised by field research that does not have experimental and control groups. Such designs are possible when one knows, with some respectable degree of certainty, what variables to study (Argyris, 1965). In this study, however, we were exploring new territory to see if we could identify the variables with the hope of eventually developing a more systematic model. As Weiss and Rein (1970) show, a process-oriented, qualitative, historical approach may be more appropriate for such a study. The payoff from naturalistic observation is primarily one of generating insights, defining dimensions, and identifying the possible interrelationships among multilevel activities. Cronbach and Gleser (1965, pp. 144–148) would describe our methods as "wideband" methods (versus narrowband). The wideband methods transmit more and richer information, but their clarity and dependability are frequently less than the narrowband methods, which are more focused. The wideband methods are especially useful for exploratory decisions, the narrowband for terminal decisions. The field of intervention and organizational change is too primitive for research that leads to terminal decisions. We are in the developmental and exploratory stages where naturalistic observations may provide important contributions.[1] Recently, in a review of personality research, Adelson stated that naturalistic concerns have been neglected. He added, "It is, by the way, a matter of some interest and of some irony, that most of the theories we lean on are derived from disciplines and scholars, e.g., psychoanalysis, ethology, Piaget, whose inductive, naturalistic modes of inquiry we neither emulate or tolerate" (Adelson, 1969, p. 218).

Admittedly, case studies can only give anecdotal, qualitative answers to these questions. However, these are necessary if more rigorous and, necessarily, more focused research is to be conducted. When we return to nature to impose on her our biases (through quantitative measurement or experimentation) we want to try to return with the variables that describe her most accurately.

---

[1]Some recent research on the use of highly sophisticated quantitative models suggests that the decision makers may prefer nonterminal decisions and may resist *valid* methods because they may take away their opportunities for psychological sources and feelings of essentiality. Chris Argyris, "Management Information Systems: The Challenge to Rationality and Emotionality," *Management Science,* in press.

Chapter two
Organization A

Organization A is a large, multinational organization that has been experiencing marked growth in the last five years. It has developed, in the same period, from an organization with an unattractive financial performance to one with an attractive financial performance. The chief executive officer (CEO), in looking ahead, became convinced that management identification, selection, and development were key challenges if the growth was to continue. Consequently he encouraged the personnel department to develop a management-by-objectives program with a heavy emphasis on management-performance approaches. The program had been in operation for several years when the CEO contacted the interventionist (Int.) to help them to generate deeper top-management commitment to a new phase of the program. The occasion he had in mind was the annual meeting to be attended by the top forty executives throughout the world.

The interventionist responded that he doubted that internal commitment to such a program could be generated in a one-day session. Also, in his experience, a genuine management-by-objectives program required basic changes in managerial policies and practices as well as in their behavior. Internal commitment is rarely developed through lectures or seminars. Finally, many performance-appraisal programs eventually faded away or caused much unintended harm to organizations because the behavior of the executives during the performance review sessions was inconsistent (and at times antagonistic) to the objective of the development of executives. To make matters more difficult, the superiors tended to be blind to the ineffectiveness of their behavior, and the subordinates tended to be careful not to discuss the subject openly (Meyer, Kay, and French, 1965).

"I know there are these problems," responded the CEO, "and that is why we need you to be there. I am sure that you can sell the executives on the importance of interpersonal relationships and dealing with people."

"Even if I were effective in selling such programs to top management," responded the interventionist, "little internal commitment would be generated. The initial enthusiasm soon would become a vivid memory while behavioral change, or even a modest increase in sensitivity, on the part of the executives would not emerge. Therefore I appreciate the invitation, but I best not accept, for your sake and for mine."

"But this meeting is important," insisted the CEO, "I think that you have much to offer us. Many of our officers have heard of you. Surely, there must be something useful you can do in a day."

After a prolonged discussion, the interventionist was able to communicate to the CEO that a useful program would be (1) to help the executives diagnose the potential problems that they saw in the program, (2) to assess the factors that would facilitate and inhibit their personal effectiveness, and, most important, (3) to sensitize the executives to the probabilities that their present leadership style and interpersonal competence may tend to inhibit or enhance the achievement of the objectives of the program.

The CEO agreed that these contributions were important. The interventionist then asked for a meeting with all the top executives in the New York area to provide them with an opportunity to question and confront the interventionist, and vice versa. If the session went well, it would mean that some of the executives attending the annual meeting would have had a genuine opportunity to accept or reject the interventionist, and if the former were the case, to provide inputs into the design of the day. The chief executive officer agreed.

The meeting was held with twelve officers present. It lasted for an hour and a half. The discussion revolved around assessing what they wished would occur at the annual meeting regarding the introduction of the management evaluation and development program as well as responding to the interventionist's views.

About a week later the officers met, without the interventionist, to decide if the latter should be invited. They tape-recorded the session, and the tape was sent to the interventionist. The interventionist listened to the tape and asked for another meeting to discuss the issues on the tape. The second meeting was held and tape-recorded.

The interventionist was then invited to the annual meeting. (More about this later.)

The discussion and analysis of organization A will be based primarily on the tape recordings of the two sessions plus the annual session.

The group and interpersonal dynamics of the executive group

On the basis of previous research, the interventionist knew that it would be possible to analyze the first two tapes in such a way as to generate a reliable and valid diagnosis of the interpersonal and group dynamics of the executive group (Argyris, 1969). The results of the analysis of the first two tapes are presented in Table 2. The interpersonal and group dynamics are similar to other executive groups which are relatively competitive (Argyris, 1966). For example, there is much owning up to ideas in such a way that the norm of conformity is the strongest (i.e., people are attempting to persuade and "sell"). There is little helping each other and a relatively high amount of overt behavior

TABLE 2   *Scores of Group A*
(expressed in percent)

	Session I $n = 100$	Session II $n = 100$
Interpersonal:		
Own i	68	65
Open i	16	15
Not helping own i	16	20
Group norms:		
Conformity i	49	51
Concern i	47	48
Individuality i	4	1
Inconsistent behavior:		
Own i—Conformity i	26	32

that does not help others to express their views (e.g., cutting people off). The norm of individuality is very weak, and no behavior is observed scorable as taking risks or contributing to the norm of trust. Note also there is no overt expression of feelings, openness to feeling, or helping others to express their feelings. As we shall see, this does not mean that the executives do not have feelings; rather they suppress them or intellectualize them while in the group.

Under these conditions it is possible to predict that there will be a tendency to postpone discussing "touchy" issues in group meetings. Discussions of such issues would probably be relegated to settings outside the group (usually in subgroups). Consequently important information about important issues would not be explored with all the members of the groups. (That would be running the risk of upsetting people, which could arouse feelings.)

Previous research also suggests that under these conditions (1) the executives will tend to emphasize the use of power and control "to get things done," and (2) they will tend to be unaware of the degree to which they cause problems for their subordinates. Their unawareness would be partially caused by the fact that few subordinates would give their superiors feedback on their impact upon them and partially caused by their conception of "strong" leadership, which is to direct and control.

The interpersonal blindness and the concept of "strong" leadership combined will tend to lead to executives who minimize the role of personal causation, i.e., the degree to which they are responsible for problems in the organization. Under these conditions individual growth will not tend to be achieved unless the executives begin by focusing on their own behavior. However, given the fact that they tend to minimize their personal causation, they will tend to resist the first step. "Changing behavior is necessary, but not for us."

The lack of awareness of the extent to which one is the origin of problems should not be interpreted to mean that the executives do not wish to know when they are an important cause of problems. Nor does it mean that the executives are unaware that they may cause human problems when they have to do something for the sake of the organization that is not popular with the participants (e.g., to fire or to demote or to reprimand someone). They are willing to own up to, to accept responsibility for, such behavior. However, under the present conditions, they tend to see the organization as the primary cause of such action. They view themselves as the agents of the organization.

The emphasis on power, the blindness to one's impact on others, the low predisposition to learn about and assess the degree to which one is an important origin (cause) of some human problems in the organization could act to make the management evaluation and development program less effective. Indeed, given these conditions, it is not too difficult to predict that their projected program would (1) not tend to facilitate individual growth and development, but would (2) probably reinforce further subordinate conformity and compliance. If these predictions are confirmed, then the subordinates would be asked to participate in a program for their development which they would experience as one that inhibits their development.

Given the analysis above, it was understandable why the clients sought an interventionist who was capable of being persuasive and "selling," who could be task-oriented, who could deal with power and authority "effectively" (i.e., not be afraid to use it in the session, but not to bring up dysfunctional consequences of power and authority), who could "shake up the troops" or generate enthusiasm in the new program. Such an interventionist fitted their view of effectiveness as being related to "strong" leadership and their willingness to let strong leaders become personally responsible for new programs. It also reduced the personal responsibility of the top executives in "selling" the program to the organization. Moreover, if the interventionist succeeded, the acceptance by the subordinates would tend to be external. They would not feel personally responsible either.

When the top group tends to be blind to their impact, when the subordinates tend to hide their feelings about the top, and, in turn, are blind about their impact on their subordinates, the conditions for the long-range effectiveness of management by objectives are not optimal.

Moreover, should this new program be "sold" to the organization, it would tend to reinforce the executives' blindness of the degree to which their philosophy of management and their behavior were important causes of the very problems that they wished to overcome. If their blindness were reinforced with simultaneous pronouncements by the executives of the importance of individual development, it would tend to influence the subordinates to suppress many of their feelings (so as not to upset the top). The loop would then be closed for the familiar phenomenon of mutually reinforced blindness and untested assumptions about superior-subordinate relationships within the system.

To cast the problem in terms of our framework, the interventionist concluded that the client system (1) was not generating valid information about its problem, and (2) was seeking an interventionist who would make choices for them and others in the organization about management-evaluation activities which would lead to a minimum internal commitment on their part to the program. These client reasons were consistent with the interpersonal and group dynamics of their system.

The interventionist concluded, therefore, that the most important contributions that he could make to the client system would be to design a confrontation session whose objectives would be to help them examine openly (1) the difficulties inherent in management-by-objectives and management-evaluation activities; (2) the difficulties they would create for and by themselves with such programs, which might lead to, at best, (3) a more realistic appraisal of the skills they would need to develop if the program were to genuinely succeed; or, at least, (4) an awareness that they are not, individually or as a system, internally committed to the values of individual development.

The interventionist's diagnosis of the clients' reactions to his first visit

We pause for a methodological note that is directed especially at the reader who is an OD professional, but which is worthy of the attention of the line executive. The interventionist is a human being and subject to making unintended distortions of reality. He should strive, therefore, to cross-check as many of his inferences as time and resources permit. Elsewhere, the writer has reviewed some possible ways that the cross validation may be made (Argyris, 1970).

In organization A, the interventionist asked a colleague to listen to the two tape recordings.[2] The colleague knew nothing about the top-management group and was not shown the interventionist's diagnoses. The colleague was

[2] Mr. Daniel Johnson.

asked to analyze the tape recordings in any way that would be meaningful to him. He was also asked to focus on two questions:

1. How did the clients seem to react to the interventionist?

2. How did the clients react to the interventionist's proposal for a confrontation session during the annual meeting?

There are several reasons why these two questions were important to the interventionist. First, he was making the inference that the clients were acting primarily positively toward him. Consequently, he believed that he was building a relationship where he could trust the validity of the information he was being given by the clients. If a disinterested colleague could show evidence that the client reaction was neither as positive nor the information as valid as the interventionist inferred, then serious questions would have to be raised about the validity of the interventionist-client relationship.

Even if the relationship was found to be an effective one, there is still the possibility that the interventionist could distort the clients' reactions to his idea for a confrontation meeting because it was his suggestion. Consequently, it was important to obtain an independent check of the clients' reactions.

Developing these types of checks is not only useful for the client-interventionist relationship; they can also provide a sounder basis for other interventionists to learn from these experiences. The intellectual and practical development of organizational development as a field depends heavily on this type of information.

The congruence of the colleague's and the interventionist's diagnoses was encouragingly high. Both agreed that there were thirty-eight units to be scored. The interventionist identified twelve comments as being favorable to him, while the colleague identified thirteen. No negative comments were identified.

Some examples were:

> "Appears to be a pro."
>
> "Has been around the track a long time."
>
> "Able to make fast, accurate, significant observations."
>
> "He's someone with integrity."

Some examples of positive comments about the confrontation session were:

> "I think that we all recognize that there is some real plus that could come out of a discussion of this type."
>
> "Awareness of our administrative deficiencies and even some of our personality deficiencies is important."
>
> "Having raw nerves exposed may be good."
>
> "We need greater openness and spontaneity."

Some comments expressed fear and reservations:

> "Could possibly be a destructive process."
>
> "Will emotional confrontation do more harm than good?"
>
> "Delicate balance with top system could be endangered."
>
> "Can organization handle effectively information about itself and not harm itself at the same time?"
>
> "Public advertisement of our defects can be harmful."

The comments provided the interventionist with important information about several different issues. First, they represented an added but indirect validation of some aspects of the diagnosis made from the scoring procedures. The comments illustrated the client system's discomfort with discussing interpersonal relationships; their fear of each other and their subordinates "if feelings were opened up"; their fear that discussion of feelings would necessarily "drain individuality," "harm people," and "make the organization less effective."

Second, the clients spoke highly of the interventionist as a person. Yet, they expressed fears about the confrontation session that he recommended because it could be full of loaded, negative evaluations. Eor example, individuals expressed concern if the interventionist, with his "great" skill, told them such things as:

"You have a closed mind."

"You're not being objective."

"Your attitude is wrong."

Several questions may be asked. If the clients understood the interventionist how could they conclude, as their examples suggest, that he would strive to behave in the attributive, evaluative manner? If they did not understand him, how did they conclude that he was a "real pro," a "man with integrity," etc.?

Perhaps the clients colluded to hide from each other and from the interventionist their true feelings. This hypothesis seemed doubtful because they were the top senior officers, and there was little external pressure on them to hire the interventionist for one day.

Another possibility was that they were saying positive things about the interventionist to be able to reject him. "He's a nice man, but not for us." This hypothesis received no observable support. Indeed several members who were laudatory in their comments about the interventionist also led a discussion confronting their peers about, "Why are we afraid of this?" or "Do we not have the strength to learn from this?" and "He never evaluated us this way; why are we saying that he will do it during the proposed meeting?"

A third possibility was that the group was projecting onto the meeting (without the interventionist) some of their own concepts of effective help and leadership. Perhaps they would evaluate each other this way. Perhaps they feared being open with each other. Perhaps they projected onto the interventionist the style of leadership that they used with their subordinates. For example, from the quantitative analysis above, we know the clients tended to be controlling and competitive. From other research we have learned that controlling leaders tend to legitimize their directiveness by viewing it as part of being strong and fulfilling the responsibilities of being in the power position. If the interventionist were hired with the view of giving him a position of power (for the day), then might they not expect him to behave toward them in a manner that was consistent with the way they behaved when they were in power? The authoritarian person is quite willing to be submissive to someone who has authority over him.

There were no data, direct or indirect, to shed light upon these questions. However, such data could be collected. The interventionist could meet with the clients and ask them questions such as:

"What did I say or do that led you to infer I would tend to help you by evaluating you or 'hitting at raw nerve'?"

"How would you relate your fears about public discussion to your interpersonal behavior?"

If such a discussion produced some evidence that the clients were indeed reflecting in their fears their style of leadership, concepts of help, and interpersonal milieu, then this would be very important for them to examine carefully. In the process of examination they would begin to reduce some of their blindness and accept more responsibility for being causal agents of the problem that they wished to overcome. Moreover, it is precisely these conditions that could help to increase the effectiveness of executive evaluation and development activities.

The interventionist asked for another meeting with the client system. The request was granted.

The confrontation during the second meeting

A confrontation is an open discussion of issues typically not discussed within the system but which are believed to be causing problems within the system. A confrontation meeting, therefore, is *not* one where individuals are being discussed or condemned for holding a position, where someone releases pent-up feelings with the intention of "getting back" at others. The objective of a confrontation is to show that an open discussion about substantive issues that have emotional components can be helpful to the individuals and to the client system.

Note: The first step is for the interventionist to obtain data in observable categories that lead the clients to make the attributions about him. Such data could provide him with insight into his impact on the clients. He could also better understand the basis for the attributions. The meeting began with the interventionist stating:

> INT.: I listened to the tape and found it fascinating and helpful. I should like to attempt to accomplish two objectives during this meeting. One is to answer some substantive questions raised about the proposed session. The other is to develop a better understanding of my relationship with you. I should like to start with this objective first, unless someone prefers differently. (*pause*)
>
> I heard on the tape such comments as, "The benefit will come when he criticizes us publicly"; "He may say, 'your attitude is all wrong'"; "Are we ready to take criticisms publicly, to have someone get to the nerve?"
>
> I should like to ask a question. What did I do or say that led you to believe that I would make such comments?

A: I thought that the CEO and you said that you wanted to tape the meetings and make critical appraisals. Didn't you say that?

INT.: Yes, I did. I am wondering what I said that led people to conclude that my appraisals would be of the type that I just described?

B: I think probably part of the problem is that we are not completely clear on your procedure. Hence, maybe there's been some jumping to conclusions from fragmentary or incomplete discussion. I was one who was concerned. I believe that we ought to go all out for this or not do anything. I prefer that we learn from you about what other organizations are doing in this area. Being examined personally or collectively is somewhat of a frightening prospect.

C: I'd just like to add one point. I think the fears relate to an article that appeared recently in the *Wall Street Journal* on T-groups. I think some of us felt that it would be perilous to have a group session that might turn out to be destructive.

INT.: I, too, can agree that a session could be destructive. My concern is what did I say, or how did you come to the conclusion that telling someone, "Now look here, you have a closed mind," is helpful?

B: I didn't say that.

D: I think pointing out people's weaknesses in a constructive manner could be helpful.

The discussion continued along the same vein. Each individual gave insight into some of his fears—the *Wall Street Journal* article, the personal assumptions they held about effective feedback, their assumptions about how aggressively they would be evaluated by their peers, and their fears about harming the authority relationships if their interpersonal "weaknesses" were exposed in front of their subordinates. These executive fears seemed valid to the interventionist.

However, no one seemed to connect these attributions

made about the interventionist with his own leadership style. The interventionist raised the issue himself.

INT.: I have a hunch which I would like to test out with you. If you think that I would be evaluative and somewhat clobbering, and if I gave you no evidence to attribute this to me, maybe your fears are based upon how you might deal with your subordinates.

E: That's an interesting hypothesis.

F: I think it's a fairly competent one.

INT.: In discussing your fears, you mentioned your concern about the impact of the program on your subordinates, on the authority relationships, etc. My immediate concern is your behavior. If you behave toward others the way that you felt I might behave toward you, it would greatly inhibit the effectiveness of your appraisal program.

B: Well, can't you reverse the logic? If the group wouldn't do it to their subordinates, why should you do it to this group?

INT.: I shouldn't and do not intend to.

B: I think I got the impression that you were going to point out defects.

INT.: Could you help me to understand where you got that impression?

B: *(silence)* I'll be darned if I know. Just looking at you! *(laughter)*[3]

The discussion continued with one individual bringing up a frequently held assumption about interpersonal relationships. If diplomacy is seen (by people like the interventionist) as closed behavior, then openness would be the opposite, which is an aggressive, somewhat punishing evaluation. "Why," asked the interventionist, "do we view openness and aggressiveness as points on the same con-

---

[3] This comment may hold important information for the interventionist. If he were to accept a relationship with the clients, it should be explored because he may be giving off nonverbal cues about which he is unaware.

tinuum?" "Do you mean that there is something in between diplomacy and aggressiveness?" some asked. "Not quite," replied the interventionist. "I mean that the other way to behave is on a different dimension." For example, openness may not be a quality in a person, but in a relationship. Therefore the test of whether a person is open is *not* simply if he is saying what he believes. The test for openness is whether he is saying what he believes in such a way that the other person can state what he believes. The test, to repeat, is in the relationship (Argyris, 1962).

The point was explored more thoroughly, and the discussion helped the clients to see that there was another set of interpersonal relationships that made sense to them. There was increased interest in learning more about the skills. In addition, some members became more aware that they were "a little scared of this new personnel appraisal system." The interventionist then added that, in his experience, many of the best-laid plans for personnel evaluation have tended to fail because of the behavior of the executives. He cited several studies to show how the executives unintentionally created, by their behavior, a higher degree of mistrust between themselves and their subordinates.

More people began to unfreeze and to see connections between the potential effectiveness of the programs and their behavior.

> G: A number of things you're saying fascinate me. In particular is the idea that we may be kidding ourselves. You see us as people who are willing to say what we believe; but we may do it in a way that could create conformity. I, for one, was unaware of this possibility. But I can see how it would be terribly important.

As support for the interventionist's diagnosis began to increase, direct confrontation of the interventionist and his methods also increased. Two of the most frequently asked questions are indicated below with the responses made by the interventionist.

The clients asked	*The interventionist responded*
1. How can you make valid inferences about us after one or two meetings?	1. *(a)* It would be difficult, but previous research and theory helps us to be more confident.
	(b) Groups are finite in their differences because individuals can handle only finite amounts of information. If every group was importantly different, people would have great difficulties.
	(c) The clients would be able constantly to confront the diagnosis and check its validity with their own experiences.
2. How can you be certain our subordinates would not leave confused if they attended the type of one-day session that you propose?	2. *(a)* We can predict that they will experience the confusion that you are experiencing.
	(b) Confusion, if it is based on genuine dilemmas, tends to challenge people's sense of competence, and if the conditions are created, it influences them to explore the issues in a more thorough manner.
	(c) The confusion can be the basis for learning if it is discussed openly.

As the questions were answered to the apparent satisfaction of the members, a bandwagon effect began to develop in favor of the program which, in turn, made it possible or encouraged others to surface their opposition to the program. This was helpful because it provided further tests of the interventionist's ability to remain consistent, deepened the questions, and increased the probability of an informed decision and the probability of higher internal commitment to whatever the decision would be.

> D: I object to the whole concept of discussing our behavior.
> A: The point is, D, that we do it all the time anyway.
> D: I don't mind doing it privately with you, but not publicly.
> A: But we do it in groups too. You and I. . . .
> D: I don't understand why we should have to look at our behavior publicly.
> INT.: There are several reasons why it would be helpful to explore your effectiveness in a group. First, a group of individuals will give you a range of views about your impact. You will not be limited to one person's view. Second, they could give you more ideas on how to alter your behavior. Third, as you learn, others are learning. Fourth, as you learn, you and others build trust in the system. Fifth, I do not know how we can give all the top executives an experience in examining their interpersonal skills in one day, without doing it in groups.
> D: Well, I don't know. If we think this is so good, let's hire someone to stay with us for a long time, not just a day.
> B: But how will we find out if it is worth doing for a longer time period?
> H: Maybe we should wait five years until the new management team has been able to jell. Don't you think we will increase our effectiveness as we get to know each other?
> INT.: If I judge from other cases that we have studied that are similar, the answer is "no." However, I do not think that your decision should be made on the basis of others' experiences. If you have serious questions, then the program should not be held.

Note: For the first time members of the client system were defending the ideas of the program.

The discussion continued with an increasing number of

individuals developing a commitment to experiment with the program. Then one executive asked if the interventionist could guarantee that no one would be asked an embarrassing question or be hurt.

> INT.: I cannot in all honesty guarantee that someone will not be asked an embarrassing question. I can tell you that I would not knowingly do it. I can also tell you that I will work hard to create a climate where people can choose to ask any question that they believe is relevant and for people to choose not to respond, if they so wish. If there are genuine fears that people have about each other's sense of concern for others, then I would caution you against this type of program. But, to repeat, I cannot guarantee something which forces me to decide how others must behave.

The comments led some people to question each other about fears toward each other. No one said that he mistrusted the group, and quite a few said that they could defend themselves if they had to. The meeting ended with the chairman saying that they would have a final vote in a day or so and inform the interventionist.

Critical episodes during the session

By replaying history and stopping it for analysis, it is possible to learn more about what happened during a session. Looking backward with the luxury of time, the session may be analyzed in terms of episodes. These episodes seemed to have distinguishable characteristics. They were not perceived as existing in natural sequences, nor were they as differentiable when they were occurring, as the analysis may suggest. Episodes greatly overlapped each other and, therefore, at times existed simultaneously.

During the first episode, the interventionist confronted

the group members about their view of the interventionist, with minimal defensiveness on his part, about their "incorrect" view of him. He first attempted to test if the group had observable data to connect his behavior with the attributions made about him. If they did have such data, it would be very important for him to learn about it. If they did not, he could legitimately ask the clients to examine their assumptions and behavior. The principle involved: The first step in understanding complex situations is for one to examine his personal causation upon the situation.

In the second episode, the interventionist attempted to help the members see that the eventual success of the personnel evaluation programs hinged on their interpersonal effectiveness; that their interpersonal effectiveness was relatively low; that to alter it they would have to explore issues typically considered taboo subjects in their group.

The reactions to this strategy varied. Some clients began the process of coping with the interventionist by asking that the group not hire him. Others attempted to induce the interventionist to accept their views of leadership "for just one meeting." Some wanted him to become evaluative and attributive. Others requested that he lecture since he showed himself "to be full of interesting ideas." The interventionist did not accept any of these roles, pointing out the danger for the clients as well as for himself. This episode generated an increasing number of clients who saw the interventionist as having certain strengths, especially under stress. They were identified as follows:

1. He knew the kind of help that he could give and the conditions that were necessary if his help was to be effective.

2. He believed strongly in his views, yet he was equally open in encouraging the generation of evidence—especially from his own behavior—that would disprove his views.

3. He behaved congruently with his views, and when he did not, he said so. He remained relatively consistent over time, under stress, and in spite of many financially attractive requests to give a more "traditional" program. He preferred that his services be rejected rather than to accept the assignment under conditions that he believed would not help the client system (even though they wanted him).

4. He was able to provide a map of the conditions under which the system would have difficulties in implementing the program. His predictions made sense to many members.

5. He emphasized individual free choice and was careful not to guarantee success—a promise which would have reduced his choice and could induce him to attempt to reduce the choices of others in order to make the program more successful.

A fourth episode was the attempt by some clients to suggest that the entire idea be postponed until they were ready to go into the program in depth. The interventionist reminded them that they were still planning to have their personnel evaluation program begin in a few months.

Next came the fears of the potential danger and the discussion to postpone the program. The interventionist acknowledged the validity of these fears for some members. He also supported their expression of these views. Simultaneously, he supported the idea of a confrontation because he saw that some of the group members were able to learn by exploring these fears, and because the executives would have to cope with these fears on the part of the subordinates when the latter came to be evaluated.

Finally, there was an attempt to make the interventionist guarantee that no one would be hurt or become confused. The interventionist responded that he could not give such a guarantee. The only guarantee that he would give would be to do his best to help make the program effective. He also would ask the others to make such a commitment. If they were unable to do so, he would then question if the program should be held.

To summarize:

As the clients	*The interventionist*
1. Described their fears	1. Accepted the fears.
2. Questioned the validity of the interventionist's methods	2. Responded rationally to their questions of validity.
3. Questioned the validity of a one-day program	3. Related the key answers to their own feelings about themselves and, thereby, their group.
4. Questioned the ethics of exploring actual behavior	4. Noted that their management-evaluation program would require them to evaluate behaviors. He also asked them to focus first on their own effectiveness before they began a program on evaluating the effectiveness of others.

As these multilevel, interdependent episodes were played out, the executives increasingly realized the value of examining their own behavior and learning more about the problems they could cause unintentionally when the personnel evaluation programs began. Moreover, as more than half the members stated overtly, the more they discussed these issues, the more they saw that the decision to develop and maintain an effective executive growth and development climate raised some very basic questions about their managerial philosophy.

The design of the annual session

The group voted unanimously to invite the interventionist to the annual program. With the help of a liaison subgroup the following design was developed:

1. The forty executives would be subdivided into three groups.

2. Each group would explore the entire personnel evaluation program. They would raise any questions that they felt were important. They would also make recommendations for the final design and implementation.

3. The interventionist (with the help of another professional)[4] would observe the dynamics of the small-group sessions as well as the substantive issues raised. During the afternoon they would present their views of the entire group.

The objectives of the day were as follows:

1. To provide the top executives with an opportunity to raise any questions they wished and to develop as much of an internal commitment to the program as possible.

2. To provide the interventionists with an opportunity to observe the group dynamics as well as the recommendations made for the final design. They could then make their final suggestions about the problems that would probably have to be overcome if the program was to succeed.

3. To provide the interventionist with further evidence to confirm or disconfirm the analysis made, to date, of the group. The data to be collected were of two kinds. The interpersonal and group dynamics of the three sessions were to be scored, as were the first sessions. The tapes

---

[4] Doctor Fred I. Steele.

would also be analyzed for the way issues were coped with and the recommendations made.

Two different types of prediction could be made ahead of time. First, the quantitative pattern presented at the outset should not change significantly. This prediction is based on the analysis that the present executives' behavioral patterns are self-maintaining and closed to learning (Argyris, 1969). Thus the two sessions with the interventionist would produce little or no change. The second prediction was that whatever recommendations the executives made about the personnel evaluation program, they would not tend to violate the behavior and norms of their system. They would not, for example, approve a program that would tend to encourage people to take interpersonal risks or to grow, because risk taking and growth are not strong norms in the system.

The results of the annual session

First, the group scores were similar to the patterns described at the outset of the chapter. Groups A and B were highly consonant with the competitive pattern, while group C was less competitive. (Groups A and B were led by competitive line executives, group C by the personnel director, who was less competitive.)

Group D represents the scores of the total group as they discussed the interventionists' comments. (For the purposes of this analysis the scores of the interventionists were not included.) The entire group became even more competitive under the confrontation and subsequent stress. Again, these findings are typical of those found in other groups. Under stress, competitive groups increase their conformity scores, their not-helping-others scores, as well as their behavior that creates inconsistencies.

These data add validity to the interventionist's initial diagnosis as well as to his two predictions that the interpersonal and group dynamics (1) are relatively stable and (2) are of such a pattern that they will tend to inhibit the effectiveness of the personnel evaluation program.

TABLE 3 *Scores of Groups A,* B, C*
(expressed in percent)

	A n = 100	B n = 100	C n = 100	D† n = 100
Interpersonal:				
Own *i*	72	65	71	64
Open *i*	14	16	17	14
Not helping own *i*	14	19	12	22
Group norms:				
Conformity *i*	50	51	48	68
Concern *i*	49	48	52	32
Individuality *i*	1	1		
Inconsistent behavior: Own *i*—				
Conformity *i*	30	32	26	42
Own *i*— Antagonism *i*				2

* This group A is different from the group described at the outset.

† D represents scores of the total group.

Two sets of anecdotal data were obtained through a content analysis of the tape recordings. First, we identified all the substantive issues to see if they were congruent or incongruent with the internal dynamics of the client system as described above. Second, we noted the reaction to these issues by the group members to see if they were coped with in ways that were consistent or inconsistent with the internal dynamics of the client system. For example:

A reaction to the program	*The response*
1. An executive said that he would feel insulted to have to fill out evaluative forms for his immediate top subordinates.	1. The chairman said, "But you missed the entire point. There is no reason why you should feel insulted. Look at the instructions and see the logic behind the program."

The individual was open about his feelings regarding the mechanics of the personal evaluation procedure (the only such comment during the entire day). The immediate response was to evaluate the individual as incorrect, to deny that he should feel insulted, and to ask him to look at the rational issues.

2. Several members spoke of their increasing tiredness at having to attend "countless boring meetings" and that they are so overworked.	2. There was no response other than for individuals to shake their heads in agreement.

No one asked the group to explore why, given that they were overworked, they permitted themselves to attend boring meetings that consumed much time.

3. An executive said, "When you have a hierarchy, you will never get open discussion because each person answers from his own vantage point. Also there is low trust, so the most honest kind of criticism has to come from an anonymous response."	3. Several executives agreed.

No one asked the question about the probability of the effectiveness of their personnel program if the most honest responses can come under conditions of anonymity. What will happen in the evaluation sessions that are planned?

The most potent episode was surfaced when individuals raised the question whether the performance appraisal forms should be filled out for the individuals at the highest levels. Some officers insisted that filling out forms for the top could be demeaning. "We know what is in our [immediate] subordinates' hearts. To interview them in a formal way seemed incongruous with our existing relationship."

Other important questions raised during this episode were, "Won't giving people a numerical grade anger them?"; "Is it safe to keep the forms on file?"; "Could not a low grade get into an individual's file and harm his career?"; "Should not the subjective reports be destroyed?"; "Would not evaluation meetings be too mechanical?" Perhaps, especially at the upper levels, one should "soften the man up first by taking him to dinner."

None of the issues were dealt with openly and thoroughly in each of the subgroups as they were raised. They did serve to alert the members, however, that they had serious reservations about the use of the formal procedures at the upper levels. In every group, almost near closing time, someone recommended a drastically reduced evaluation activity for the top executives. The full program was recommended for the lower-level executives.

The interventionists attempted to confront the group on their assumption that a process that would not be helpful at the highest levels would be helpful at the lower levels. The group members resisted the implication that the conditions for effective evaluation were basically similar at all levels. Some interesting rationalizations were presented to explain the exclusion of the top executives from the evaluation procedures. Some executives argued that the informality and congeniality of the home office could be harmed by the introduction of a formal set of procedures. Some of those making this point were the same individuals who were arguing previously against informality and un-structured programs at the annual meeting because it could harm relationships. Others felt that the younger executives should go through the appraisal processes as part of an initiation rite. Finally, others indicated that going through the evaluation procedures would act as a useful selection device to see who can take the authoritar-ian structure that must exist in business. For example:

> A: I'd like to make a comment. There is a high degree of co-hesion in the management of this company. That goes in spades for the home office. It is a rather intimate office. I think that there may be some fear that these [close] relationships might be destroyed if we formalize the rating process.
>
> INT. A: I agree with you on the danger. But I would suggest that the danger exists at all levels.
>
> B: [The men who succeed have power]—How does a man get that right to power? He has been graded, evaluated, taken apart, and put back together again. Why should the young people object to going through the same process that we went through?
>
> INT. B: Like an initiation rite?
>
> B: Yes.
>
> C: We've been through it a million times.
>
> INT. B: Is it worth it to get revenge on them for what you had to go through? *(laughter)*
>
> D: Business has certain ground rules. Some people can't or don't want to adapt. Business is not conducted on demo-cratic principles. It is an authoritarian structure. All right, up to a certain point we go through [an evaluation] by our

superiors as to whether we are material for the top of the pyramid. Once [an individual] is past the point where we know he is [acceptable], then he no longer needs to be evaluated so closely.

One executive owned up, "I guess somehow we decided these forms were for the troops. Officers to the left and other ranks to the right."

The next several speakers defended their recommendations on the grounds that the lower-level men were younger men and had to be helped to develop "properly." Then one executive said:

A: I frankly find it embarrassing to sit down with a man and score him plus and minus. This can get pretty ridiculous.

INT. B: Wouldn't that also be true for the younger men?

A: No, for two reasons. One, you don't see him often.

B: But what does that? . . .

A: They need to be told.

INT. A: Are you saying that you agree to communicate to the other executives that there are the high- and the low-status men? The low-status men need development, but not the high-status men?

A: This is true. *(laughter)* When you reach a certain age, you've got a lower tolerance to these things. But the younger men need to be guided and molded.

INT. B: Perhaps one issue is whether the evaluation program is to be conceived as a control program rather than one for learning and growth. These are two significantly different objectives. They call for different behavior on the part of the superior and the subordinate.

At this time, the meeting had to come to an end. The group spokesman summarized their views. The predominant theme was that management performance, evaluation, and development was a much more complicated process than they had anticipated. They also realized they were not ready to introduce the new program into the organization. Finally as one man said, "The most disturbing lesson is that we have to look at ourselves more than we thought we would have to."

SUMMARY

A. Dynamics of the client system

1. The executive system was characterized by much owning up to ideas in a way that reinforced, first, the norm of conformity and, second, the norm of concern for ideas. Not helping others and scores of inconsistent behavior were relatively high. Experimenting, expression of feelings, and helping others were rarely observed. The norms of individuality and trust were very weak.

2. Under stress the system magnified the conformity, not helping others, and the inconsistent behavior.

3. The patterns of interpersonal and group dynamics were stable. The patterns ascertained during the first days were replicated three months later at the annual meeting.

4. The variance of individual member scores was not shown, but it was not large. Most of the individuals who spoke manifested a pattern similar to the group scores.

B. Prognosis for effective intervention

1. Effective intervention would be very difficult because the client system

(a) Did not sanction experimenting or expression of feelings, individuality, and trust.

(b) Did not encourage the awareness of personal causation.

(c) Did sanction the concept that effective leadership is controlling, directive leadership.

(d) Did sanction the concept that effective human relationships were formed around the qualities of intellectual articulateness, competitiveness, and the appropriate suppression of feelings about self and others (called "diplomacy"). Therefore "openness" tended to mean the release of pent-up feelings which, in turn, was usually correlated with aggressive, punishing behavior.

(e) Did not encourage development of cognitive maps about, nor the development of skills for, interpersonal competence, effective groups or intergroups.

(f) Did create a milieu which resulted in the individuals having little confidence in themselves and in other group members to change their behavior.

(g) Did create norms where changes toward increasing interpersonal competence were defended against by polarizing the differences (i.e., soft versus hard leadership) and by emphasizing the lack of useful cognitive maps to point the directions for effective increase in interpersonal competence *and* maps to show the type of organizational structures and administrative controls that would support more authentic relationships.

In summary, the factors that the client system discouraged supported the factors that it encouraged, which, in turn, supported the present makeup of the system, which was precisely what required modification.

C. Findings regarding the processes of intervention

1. It was possible to adhere to the primary tasks of generating valid information, free choice, and internal

commitment in a client system where the prognosis described above was pessimistic. Indeed, the interventionist's consistent adherence to these tasks created learning opportunities for the client system that were helpful to them beyond what they had expected from a very short relationship.

2. Adhering to the primary tasks did not mean that the interventionist took primarily a passive or minimally directive stance vis-à-vis the clients. The interventionist was continuously active in generating data, confronting issues, questioning the validity of some of the most basic assumptions held by the clients, and in making predictions about the client system as well as the probable effectiveness of the program being planned.

Two basic supports and springboards for the active role were the interventionist's clarity and commitment to his position as well as his use of the research literature to make statements that could be tested within the group. Concerning the former, the interventionist had a relatively well thought through map of his values and the processes that were effective. He held these views with confidence, yet with awareness of their limitations. This did not mean he would not be open to confrontation and disconfirmation. Indeed, the interventionist encouraged confrontation of himself and his views. He used the resulting here-and-now dialogue as a basis for continual testing of his views and of learning from the clients.

High confidence in one's ideas combined with high openness to disconfirmation may, therefore, be more effective.

Some examples of the high confidence–high openness to disconfirmation occurred when the interventionist made the following statements and encouraged the clients to challenge him.

1. Internal commitment on the part of all executives

was necessary for the long-run effectiveness of the managerial performance evaluation and development program.

2. Internal commitment was rarely—if ever—generated within skeptical audiences by well-articulated lectures.

3. Valid diagnosis of the interpersonal and group dynamics could be made on the basis of the tape analysis of a few ongoing group sessions.

4. Valid predictions could be made about behavior of the group during the meetings with the interventionist, without the interventionist, and even after they accepted the interventionist's views on the issues being predicted. For example:

(a) Threatening but relevant interpersonal issues would not be discussed openly.

(b) Power and authority would be used to accomplish programs.

(c) Blindness existed about impact people were having on each other.

These predictions were made during the first session. The interventionist was then able to provide evidence of his predictions through quantitative analysis of tapes of subsequent meetings and through the identification of the way people dealt with each other (e.g., not dealing with the feelings Mr. A had of being insulted, the frequent "selling" behavior during the meetings, the conclusion generated by the group that would make the new evaluation and development program one of control and conformity-producing activity).

The underlying assumptions made by the interventionist in shaping his share of the client-interventionist process was that he should strive continuously to generate valid information and free choice, and help the clients to generate internal commitment to their choices. These conditions can best be achieved if the interventionists help the clients to produce information that is *directly observable, minimally evaluative, minimally attributive,* and *minimally inconsistent.*

Clients, however, given their interpersonal and group dynamics, were usually highly evaluative, attributive, and inconsistent, and used inferred categories. One cannot focus on all these issues in a few sessions. The interventionist chose to focus on generating valid information because it was the necessary precondition to free choice and internal commitment.

Therefore the interventionist, whenever possible, illustrated his view by relating it to actual behavior either on tapes or on here-and-now behavior during the meetings.

Briefly, the interventionist asked the clients to discuss their attributions of him by giving him some observable data from which they made their attributions. The clients were unable to do so. However, in the process of self-examination they focused on such factors as the article in the *Wall Street Journal,* the stories they had heard about T-groups, their fear of what their peers would say and think, etc.

The interventionist was careful not to attempt to disprove their view of him (which he believed to be invalid), but to focus their attention on learning from the "mis-diagnosis." Thus he helped the clients to consider the possibility that they projected onto him (a person about whom they admitted they had little data) much of their own behavior (i.e., evaluative, punishing); that they could also be describing how they probably behave with their subordinates; and that their willingness to be evaluated by them could indicate that they require their subordinates to take a relatively dependent role vis-à-vis them.

As an increasing number of clients agreed, they generated their own data to illustrate the interventionist's hypotheses. As agreement increased, those who resisted covertly became more overt in their resistance. They began to challenge the interventionist by surfacing some of their more basic and less consciously articulated assumptions about subordinates and about effective human relationships. An example of the former was the assumption that subordinates had to be controlled if they were "to grow properly." An example of the latter was that there were only polarized choices, such as hard versus soft leadership and diplomatic versus hostile relationships.

The interventionist was able to present other alternatives or show the inconsistency of their position (e.g., they were so soft on confronting interpersonal and group issues that they frequently attended meetings that they called boring and dull, even though they complained that they were overloaded with work).

As the questions were answered, more clients began to understand the position taken by the interventionist and increased their willingness to experiment with it. The final questions were those which asked if the assurances could be given that no one would be hurt and that the superior-subordinate relationships would not be harmed. The interventionist responded by providing only the assurance of what he would do and by noting that the only ones who could develop the assurances they sought were themselves. Again the emphasis was on free choice and personal causation.

The clients then voted unanimously to invite the interventionists for the day. The session provided them with much evidence that their philosophy of values and their behavior were critical variables in the long-run effectiveness of the program.

Chapter three
Organization B

The focus in this case is upon the top ten executives of a manufacturing organization that also had plants in Europe and South America. The three highest-level officers (president, executive vice-president, and vice-president–treasurer) had developed an interest in Douglas McGregor's view of theory Y management. They had concluded, after careful study, that the most important barriers to growth and profits in their firm had occurred because, in the past, the organization had been managed in a highly authoritarian and paternalistic manner. The result was a management increasingly dependent-oriented and stability-shackled at all levels, which inhibited not only corporate growth and innovation, but the attraction and development of younger management.

The top three executives had attended laboratory programs of the NTL Institute for Applied Behavioral Science. They found these learning experiences very helpful and offered them to others in the corporation. Three other top officers attended laboratories and found them helpful. They, too, became proponents of theory Y management principles. Another of the top executives, who found the T-group experience valuable, was ambivalent about the application of some of the implicit values in their organizational setting. Three other executives were for different reasons (which will be explored below) against the application of laboratory learning values and theory Y management principles in their organization.

The top three executives believed that it would be inconsistent with theory Y principles to attempt to force others to accept theory Y. However, they felt equally disenchanted with the prospect that the organization be managed with the top officers using different or antagonistic managerial principles. They were concerned not only about problems that this might create at the top, but about the impact of the "split" in management philosophy upon the executives below.

Is it possible, they asked the interventionist, to develop a one-day program for the top group where this dilemma would begin to be confronted and discussed? They did not want to coerce anyone into theory Y, nor did they want to lose any top executives out of anger for being coerced toward managerial principles that did not make sense to them. On the other hand, they did want to generate a lively ongoing dialogue where all views were discussed. This, they hoped, would result in a clearer map for the entire top management as to what should be the eventual philosophy of the organization. Even though, in their view, the present house-divided situation existed for too long a time (one year), they were not asking for conclusive results in the immediate future. They simply wanted to see signs of dialogue and progress in problem solving.

The dynamics of the top group

Tape recordings of two regular meetings of the top group were sent to the interventionist. He analyzed them to ascertain the kind of interpersonal and group dynamics that existed within the group. The results, shown in Table 4, suggested that the group was similar to other groups studied in large organizations that were not characterized by a high degree of competitiveness (Argyris, 1969). Thus they tended to own up to ideas in a way that made the norm of concern for ideas stronger than the norm for conformity. Openness was slightly higher than in the group in organiza-

TABLE 4   *Scores for Group B*
(expressed in percent)

	Session I n = 100	Session II n = 100
Interpersonal:		
Own *i*	64	66
Open *i*	20	18
Helping others	8	8
Not helping others	8	8
Norms:		
Concern *i*	51	53
Conformity *i*	43	39
Individuality *i*	6	8
Inconsistent behavior:		
Own *i*—Concern *i*	19	18

tion A. Not helping others was significantly lower while, for the first time, we note some helping-others scores. At the norms level concern was higher than conformity, and individuality was more powerful than in organization A. Inconsistent behavior was also somewhat lower.

One might wonder why the scores would not be different, since the top three executives had attended and had found their laboratory experiences very valuable. Why was there not more effective behavior observed than is typical for groups, none of whose members have profited from laboratory education? Interviews with the individuals involved and analysis of the quantitative data suggest an answer already noted in other studies. The use of more authentic behavior is dependent upon a reciprocal relationship. It is difficult for an individual to behave authentically by himself. Authenticity is an interpersonal phenomenon that requires a reciprocal relationship. Since the group was split, the executives hesitated to utilize their more effective behavior. As we shall see, such behavior tended to frustrate and upset those who were against and those who were ambivalent toward change. It is interesting to note that all but one of the helping-others scores were made by the Y-oriented executives to executives with similar views. The same was true for individuality scores.

The results emphasize a dilemma all systems may face that consider developing a philosophy of management that is different from the one most prevalent now (theory X) and which has as one of its basic tenets the importance of free choice. If one cannot order theory Y, how can one influence those who insist on being adherents of theory X to, at least, experiment with theory Y types of behavior or policies? Is an organization doomed to a split with the destructive divisiveness that would occur at all levels?

The difference in views

No individual (or organization) is completely X-oriented or Y-oriented. Indeed, as pointed out in the introduction, behavioral scientists have long argued that each orientation has advantages under different conditions. For analytical purposes, however, let us divide the client group into three subgroups. Subgroup 1 contained four members who were strongly oriented toward theory Y, while in the second group three executives were equally strongly oriented toward theory X. Subgroup 3 contained individuals who were ambivalent or uncommitted. (In actuality all groups were ambivalent. As we shall see, this analytical differentiation oversimplifies reality because, under certain conditions, the theory Y group behaved closed to theory X values and vice versa.)

The division in management philosophy

One way to begin to explore the problem that existed in this client system is to examine the position of each disagreeing subgroup.

Group 2 contained three key officers. Their primary questions about theory Y were described during a meeting where the function of organizational development (OD) was being discussed and designed. They objected to OD because:

1. Theory Ẏ is not action-oriented, not profit conscious. "Our meetings can get bogged down in analyzing group process to the detriment of getting the job done. It is a lot of talk and no action."

2. OD focuses too much on process and feelings. Focus-

ing on process means that people are asked to talk about issues that embarrass them. This could create disunity and tension within the top group.

A focus on process leads to a predisposition to over-analyze behavior and make mountains out of mole hills. As one man put it:"There is all this talk about lack of trust. I don't feel it. We're all honest. I trust you and I am sure that you trust me. All of us are working for the common good."

Moreover, the emphasis on feelings makes people even more tense. If the organization is not careful, it can create an emotional situation that is like a runaway locomotive. This may occur because as individuals become emotional they tend to distort reality, which upsets others, who in turn distort reality, thereby setting off a circular and de-structive process.

3. Theory Y leads to soft management. There is an emphasis on delegating responsibility and letting people go their own way even though what they are doing is ineffective. There seems to be a fear of getting rid of deadwood.

4. The final argument surfaced only after some discussion. The people who adhered to theory X expressed a belief that to ask for help, to talk openly about being confused, to explore feelings, all these activities were signs of weakness. Leaders had to be strong. If one had doubts, they should not be surfaced. If they are discussed, it should be in private, with a very close friend, preferably one not associated with the organization.

Group 1 members had difficulties with these arguments. Their views could be summarized as follows:

1. Theory Y and OD are very much action-oriented. We are changing our management style because it has led to lower profits and poor performance. If it can be shown

that the appropriate and effective use of OD is inimical to our survival and health, then we would seriously question its inclusion in our organization.

There may be, especially during the early stages, many group discussions because an organization has much to work through to unfreeze and to correct the excess managerial baggage that it had been carrying. (To this the writer would like to add that there is much unnecessary talk and meetings in theory X organizations. Consider the innumerable "dry runs," the small clique meetings, the rumor system, as well as the countless numbers of ineffective group meetings so roundly condemned by many executives.)

2. Focusing on interpersonal group process may be embarrassing and difficult, but this will decrease as the members become more competent in this area. A focus on group process tends to create disunity when such a process is seen as being illegitimate. Otherwise, an effective focus on process tends to surface disunity, but not create it.

3. It is true that a focus on process can lead to an overanalysis of behavior. This is especially true during the early stages. However, as competence increases, the overanalyses should be confronted and reduced. People are more in control of the group meetings they attend rather than prisoners of meetings, as is presently the case.

Again the writer would add that in a theory X organization many hours are spent in overanalysis of issues. The difference is that it tends to be done privately, over lunches, or during a drink and is always cloaked in such language as "planning," "getting up to date," "catching up," "clarifying problems," and "developing appropriate strategies to win."

4. Theory Y does not lead to soft management. If it does, we are performing it incorrectly. We found that our organization became soft under theory X, while the only ones

who were "strong" were a few top people. As the organization became soft and ineffective, the strong leaders resisted firing people and indeed tended not to look squarely at the issue of deadwood in the organization.

To ask for help, to express doubts, to be open about one's confusion is not being weak. We had found it requires a lot of confidence in ourselves and in others to talk about these issues. If this is all we talked about, then it would indeed be a sign of weakness.

Preferred methods of coping with differences

Group 2's preferred mode of coping with the conflict was not to talk about it. They would prefer to "get on with the job." They believed that the split in views was not having a derogatory effect on their subordinates. Each executive, they insisted, could choose whatever leadership style he wished. Since they were all loyal, no problems should arise.

When asked why they would not discuss with the other group issues about theory Y, they responded that subordinates should not confront their superiors. Since group 1 was composed of the most powerful executives, then local option would be the best alternative for them. When asked about the possibility of division among the executive team, two members suggested that if this was a major concern then, "Let the top management order all of us to behave more in line with theory Y." "But," continued another member, "I don't think they would do it, because down deep they know this participation nonsense is nonsense. It's a game they're playing which will pass." Another stated, "It is management's job to rule, to be the nosecone on the ship."

Group 1, on the other hand, preferred a dialogue and

confrontation. They believed that, if the individuals had a constructive intent and were open to genuine influence, then the issues could be worked out and solved. Also a continuous dialogue would help all concerned develop more complete and consistent maps of the management philosophy and its action complications. They did not mind the local-option strategy as long as it was seen as an experiment where systematic data were collected on the effectiveness of all the different styles. They questioned seriously that the managers below the top level were not being confused and inhibited by the split in philosophy at the upper levels. They could give many examples where subordinates several levels below have talked about the confusion and division within the organization.

In short, group 2 wished to forget about the issue, while group 1 wished to confront it and develop an ongoing dialogue. After several inquiries from group 1, group 2 agreed to meet to discuss the issues as long as there was no T-group, no group process, no discussion of feelings.

It was at this point that the interventionist was asked to design and manage such a meeting.

The design of the confrontation meeting

The interventionist accepted the concept of the meeting because it represented an important challenge. Is it possible to begin to unfreeze individuals without having a priori the freedom to explore emotional, interpersonal, or group issues? How much can one unfreeze individuals to consider the validity of exploring emotion without utilizing the methods of experiential learning usually related to T-groups? At the moment, the major technology used to expose people to the laboratory values is laboratory technology. But, this means that individuals cannot explore the issues they question without being placed in a situation which they reject in the first place.

The interventionist did not expect to answer this question in one experience. However, such an experience, which is rarely available, may help to identify some of the factors that could facilitate the process, thereby leading to more systematic research and more disciplined practice.

The initial strategy during the meeting was developed from Lewin's field-force analysis and his concept of quasi-stationary equilibria. The first step was to identify and, it was hoped, reduce the restraining forces. Simultaneously, the interventionist took the position that he would not do anything to support the forces for divisiveness with the top-management group and the organization. Thus the local option was not an option unless it could be studied and evaluated. To put this another way, as in organization A, the assumption was made that the interventionist could be effective if he helped the clients first to generate valid information and then to try to create conditions for informed choice and internal commitment about leadership styles and philosophy of management.

A brief description of some of the processes during the meeting [5]

1. Identifying the restraining forces   The first step taken in the meeting was to ask for a list of questions individuals had that they wished to discuss during the (eight-hour) period available. The first question asked was, "What does OD mean?" The second one was, "Are T-groups and OD the same?" Interventionist B helped to surface the ques-

[5] The interventionist was assisted by Doctor Clayton Alderfer.

tion, "Does an emphasis on OD smother technical competence?"

Seeing that these questions were accepted with genuine interest by the interventionists, the members of group 2 plus several of those who were ambivalent raised all the concerns, fears, and biases they had about OD. Since they have been listed above, they will not be repeated.

The three "resisting" key executives then asked if the top three *really* knew what they had bought, and they wanted to know if theory Y would be "shoved down people's throats." EVP (the executive vice-president) responded that he knew what he had bought for himself. Before, he was a directive, controlling leader who never knew much inner peace nor helped people to develop. He believed that he had changed somewhat and that he had experienced a greater sense of inner peace, yet he continued to work as productively as ever.

Several commented that they doubted that people could really change. When asked if they felt that EVP had changed, those who had been there for three years and knew the "old" EVP agreed that changes had occurred. However, some added they felt that he had become softer.

Before the EVP could respond, another executive added that in the last year there had been an overemphasis on group process analysis. He cited an example where the VPT (vice-president–treasurer) had suddenly begun a process discussion with a room full of executives who had never had such an experience before.

The interventionist helped the members to discuss the incident thoroughly. Agreement was reached (and led by VPT) that his intervention was abrupt and ineffectively made. VPT said that he did not wish to do this again; nor, on the other hand, did he wish to be in meetings where the "tension is so thick you can cut it, yet no one is talking about it."

2. *Exploring inconsistencies* The interventionist then helped the total top group to explore some inconsistencies:

On the one hand XA members said:	*On the other hand the interventionist pointed out:*
(a) Theory Y adherents were soft, and this had led to reduced profits.	*(a)* Theory X adherents have not been able to confront the top three executives who they believed were responsible for a reduction in profits. Theory X executives were "soft" on their superiors.
(b) XA executives insisted that they were hard-nosed.	*(b)* Yet they openly stated that they feared feelings and interpersonal relationships. They also feared OD people, whom they called "headshrinkers."
(c) Hard-nosed management led to hard-nosed subordinates.	*(c)* Hard-nosed superiors usually developed soft-nosed subordinates.
(d) Hard-nosed managers were decisive and forceful.	*(d)* What was so difficult about being decisive and forceful if one had the power and simultaneously discouraged or disallowed feedback on his leadership style?
(e) XA adherents said that trust was already high in the organization.	*(e)* XA adherents expressed a high mistrust of YB adherents.
(f) XA adherents insisted there were no conflicts or tensions among managers.	*(f)* Many younger executives reported conflicts and tensions, but were conflicted about surfacing them.
(g) XA adherents insisted OD programs be postponed until philosophy of management was clarified.	*(g)* XA adherents also insisted on local option for management philosophy.

(h) XA adherents wanted proof that theory Y would work before they would adopt it.

(h) This made XA adherents soft on experimentation and risk taking.

Each inconsistency was only partially worked through. As progress was being made in one area, the individuals would turn to another. When it became evident that this, too, would lead to an inconsistency, again changes were made. However, the number of changes that could be made in the direction of the discussion were limited. At some point the underlying problem of inconsistency would have to be faced.

3. *The danger of creating defensiveness and win-lose dynamics*
The discussion, by the way, was tiring on the interventionists because the dialogue was primarily in win-lose terms. The XA adherents perceived the interventionists as the "enemy" to be defeated. The reader may wonder what kind of progress can occur if the overt process is one of challenging the XA adherents (as well as the theory YB adherents) by pointing up inconsistencies in their position. Would they not eventually feel "backed into a corner?" An analysis of the tapes suggests that the XA adherents did have, from time to time, such feelings. However, in interviews later they reported that the more they became aware of the process, the more they realized that they were as much, if not more, responsible for backing themselves into a corner. Initially this generated feeling that the interventionists were "shrewd," subtly manipulative, and not to be trusted. However, these attributions were difficult to maintain since the interventionists rarely behaved this way; or when they did, they owned up to it or accepted confrontation of their behavior. Finally, many of the ambivalents whom the XA's respected as being "strong" were

agreeing with the interventionists. Apparently the strategy of pointing up inconsistencies, especially with here-and-now behavior, may have helped to begin to unfreeze the situation.

4. Answering questions authoritatively, but not authoritarianly
Another skill manifested by the interventionists was their willingness and ability to answer questions authoritatively (not authoritarianly) and consistently. This impressed the XA executives, partially because rationality and consistency are respected in the XA world. Another possible factor may be that aggressive, counterdependent executives may be frightened by passive, withdrawing individuals because part of the motivation for aggression may be to become close to others (perhaps so close that one does not see one's destructive impact). Thus an adversary who withdraws and acts confused provides the XA individual with feelings that he is making someone dependent upon him and possibly hurting him. These feelings are unacceptable to the XA individual since his fighting is a way of getting close to people and denying his own needs to be dependent (a mode of reaction usually identified as "counterdependence"). Rather than face these issues he strikes hard at others who act confused or withdraw by labeling them as weak and, therefore, unworthy of leadership positions.

5. The positive effect of confrontation for the highly competitive-resistant client A somewhat confronting interventionist may help to reduce the anxiety of the competitive-resistant client, because his willingness to keep jousting permits the competitive client to feel close and that his aggressiveness is not causing rejection. The important point is for the interventionists to confront and joust and yet minimize the use of win-lose language or tactics. The interventionists may attempt to be as unambiguous as they can be about the values that they support and to behave in ways that are consistent with these values, even though (in the eyes of those who see the situation in win-lose terms) doing so would mean that they would lose.

For example, the interventionists, in these sessions, valued valid information, free choice, and internal commitment. Valid information, in turn, was seen as helpful to the client when it was given in the form of directly observable categories that were minimally evaluative, attributive, and inconsistent. The interventionists would, therefore, attempt to "pin down" any attribution by asking for examples, especially in the here-and-now, which would be the most easily directly verifiable events. They attempted to be minimally evaluative and minimally attributive with those who believed strongly in XA, even though the XA's behaved toward the interventionists in highly evaluative ways. The interventionists attempted to behave in ways that generated valid information from and for either "side." The interventionists were successful when they were able to create processes that helped to get all relevant views surfaced with minimal distortion.

There were times, however, when the interventionists became evaluative and attributive. For example, some clients attributed manipulative motives to the interventionists. The interventionist then asked *(a)* "What have I said or done that would lead you to infer that my motive was to manipulate you?" and/or *(b)* "How do others view me along this issue of manipulation?" In the case of the former, the individuals making the attribution were unable to generate any directly observable data, yet they continued to attribute the motives to the interventionist. In the case of the latter, the XA's would receive little support, or those who supported them could not provide any directly verifiable behavior.

An episode may help to illustrate the point. Two individuals maintained that the YB adherents and the interventionists recommended that the best way to deal with people was to "soft-soap them," "keep them smiling," "be nice to them and don't upset them." When asked to give illustrations of episodes where the adherents said or behaved in accordance with the attributions, they were unable to do so. The YB adherents and the interventionists repeated their position that they were not interested in a "kid-glove" philosophy which they saw as a manipulative philosophy. They also invited feedback of examples when they were behaving in ways that were in contradiction to their views. XA attributers ignored the invitation, but continued to maintain that YB was "being nice to people," etc. At one point, one of the interventionists said, "We have attempted to do our best to give you our view of our intentions. You keep questioning their validity without presenting any of the evidence that you say exists. Now *(becomes angry)* let me say this once more.   ." *(stated his position)* and then said, "Let me be unambiguously clear. I am fed up with being misrepresented."

Some interventionists believe that aggressive, somewhat hostile interventions like these should not be made. The writer agrees in principle but believes that there are certain conditions under which they may be helpful.

As we have seen, and will continue to see in case C, one of the important issues revolving around YB is that of being soft in dealing with people. Those who are most concerned about this issue tend to be those whose normal style is aggressive, competitive, striving to win, and fighting never to lose.

One possible reason for this behavior is that the aggressive, competitive people may have received much feedback (especially during adolescence and early manhood) that their behavior controls and threatens others. If this is the case, then these aggressive people realize that they run the risk of hurting and/or being isolated from many human beings because of their natural style of behavior. This isolation could be threatening. If they are unable to alter their aggressive and competitive style, then they are in a bind. One way to cope with this is to seek out relationships with people who do not collapse under aggressive and competitive behavior. Therefore they may feel closest to, most comfortable with, least defensive toward, and hear most accurately those substantive messages that are accompanied by enough aggressiveness and competitiveness to confirm to them that the other is not weak.

In other words competitive, aggressive individuals may reduce their defensiveness and hear certain messages after they have experienced that the other will not permit himself to be endlessly badgered and that he is quite capable of retaliating.

6. Avoiding escalation of win-lose dynamics   One danger with this strategy is that it may escalate to become a shouting match where more heat than light is generated. The interventionist can reduce this probability in several ways.

(a) It is important for the interventionist to have done the best that he could to negate the necessity for him to violate his values. For example, in the case above, the interventionist asked several times for examples of his behavior that led the other to attribute the incorrect motivation to him. Also, he asked the individual to try to reduce the condemnatory evaluative comments because it made it difficult for him not to become defensive. The interventionist pointed out several times how the aggressive, clobbering behavior tended to make it more difficult to have effective communication.

(b) If the interventionist had done his best to be aware

of his responsibility for ineffective communication and has, on his part, minimized such behavior, then it will tend to be easier to become agressive without disliking himself or the other, or seeking to win out. If the other individual responds positively (as in the case above), there is no need for the interventionist to continue (since his objective is not to win).

(c) Associated with minimal guilt about one's own behavior and minimal anger toward the other's is the ability to own up to the defensive, destructive aspects of his behavior and not to justify them. Thus if the other responds with, "Well, all you're doing is getting as badgering as you say I am," the interventionist is able to respond in effect, "Yes, I agree with you. I prefer not to continue it because, as you point out, it is not helpful; but I see no other way to deal with this situation."

7. Overcoming the idealization of the interventionist by the client
There are some clients who tend to idealize any expert and expect him to be perfect. The more the expert seems to behave effectively, especially under difficult conditions, the more he becomes admired, and the more he is threatening to such clients. The interventionist is admired because he manifests the competence the clients may wish they had. However, the more he is able to manifest this competence under difficult conditions, the more the clients may become defensive, because they see the gap between where they are and where they wish to be as becoming greater.

These clients tend to react to an intervention like the one described above with a certain degree of glee and relief. The interventionist became defensive! He, too, can be human. The relief may occur because the "error" helps to reduce their idealization of the interventionist and, therefore, their own gap between actual and ideal behavior.

The writer has found it helpful in interacting with these types of clients to own up to his defensiveness and then ask what it is that he said that implied that he or others should never get defensive, especially if they feel they are being manipulated and badgered, and their messages distorted. A discussion of this question rarely produces any such messages. The clients realize that their views may be a projection of the very high level of aspiration that they require of themselves. If, on the other hand, valid examples are produced, then the interventionist learns and can correct his miscommunications.

Two other conditions under which evaluative and hostile interventions may be relevant may be identified. In the writer's experience such an intervention may be viewed as more appropriate in a meeting where YB philosophy and behavior are not sanctioned by design. The reader may recall that this was the case in this meeting. The XA adherents had asked to minimize YB conditions.

The intervention may also be relevant when the relationship is a very short one. If the meeting is for only one day, then it is important for the interventionist to get his views legitimately represented during the discussion that follows *after* he leaves. Otherwise, defensive members can continue to make unsubstantiated attributions that could help to immobilize a group. A dramatic intervention is difficult to suppress from individuals' memories.

8. Further outcomes from remaining consistent under stress
The second consequence of remaining consistent—especially under conditions of aggression and mistrust—was that the ambivalents were able to begin to unfreeze their position and show a willingness to experiment with the views that, up to this point, they had opposed. Although

the contagion dynamics are not clear to the writer, several hypotheses come to mind.

(a) The interventionists were asking for experimentation and assessment, not for agreement or acceptance. The ambivalents were, therefore, encouraged to explore their ambivalence rather than deny it.

(b) The ability of the interventionists to be consistent under stress helped the ambivalents to reduce their fears that under stress a YB-oriented individual must immediately turn to XA (which would then make him an inconsistent individual). They, too, might be able to develop these skills someday.

The ability of the interventionists, however, may lead some clients to feel a temporary state of admiration and dependence upon them. The ambivalents would be willing to experiment because of their faith in the interventionists' abilities.

Perhaps this can be an effective way to begin to get a group to consider experimentation with new behavior when they are not in a laboratory setting. In an XA setting, the responsibility for risk taking may be more legitimately assumed by or related to the interventionists. If the ambivalents were willing to experiment, and if the experiments produced success, then the ambivalents could begin to accept more responsibility for the new behavior. If this process of transition from externally induced to internally induced experimentation is to be effective, it is important that the initial dependence upon the interventionist be surfaced and accepted, albeit as a temporary phenomenon to make experimental behavior legitimate in an XA world.

It may be, therefore, that an interventionist, especially in a session with high constraints, could influence the ambivalents, who in turn could help to influence the individuals with more extreme positions. However, to remain consistent with the analysis, the interventions must be aimed at those creating the confrontation and be genuine attempts to influence them. If the ambivalents had valid reason to believe that the interventionist was really "playing to them" while talking to the extremists, then they would have valid reasons to mistrust him. To put it another way, the ambivalents may be ambivalents partially because they believed in some of the values but doubted their applicability especially under stress. If they could see that individuals (e.g., interventionists) could be consistent with the new values and responsible to the client system, then they might be more willing to unfreeze.

This is the process that seemed to occur during the meeting. The more extreme antagonists presented the overt resistance. As the interventionists showed that they could remain consistent (e.g., they were not attempting to persuade the clients to accept one theory over another, but were asking for the design of opportunities to experiment and generate valid information), the ambivalents became more overtly supporting. By the end of the meeting all but two individuals had agreed to a study of the top group. The study would diagnose the regularly scheduled top-management meetings to ascertain the degree of openness, risk taking, trust, etc. The remaining two also agreed to the study, but the interventionist doubted that these two clients were internally committed to generating valid data. The interventionists stated this and invited them and others to confront the study at any time that they felt it to be necessary.

9. Examples of different types of confrontation Let us turn to some specimens of the interventionists' behavior during the meeting that illustrate how the interventionists confronted the issues.

(a) Asking for directly verifiable information by requesting examples or identifying individual behavior (within the group).

> A: It constantly comes up. Somebody says,"Well you said this; what did you mean by that?" The inference is that something different was meant than what was said. I can give examples. It is disturbing to people because we blow it all out of proportion.
> INT.: I, too, would be concerned if issues were blown out of proportion. Could you give us an example?
> A: Well, let's see, huh, huh, it's hard to think of one. *(silence)*
> INT.: Perhaps an example has or may occur during today's meeting. If so, we could use that to help us.

(b) Confronting by bringing out inconsistency. Executive B maintained that trust is very high in the group despite questions raised by others and his inability to give illustrations.

> B: I don't think there is mistrust. I have never witnessed a lack of trust in this group. There has *never* come to my mind *any* element of mistrust.
> INT.: Wait a minute. I do not see it that way. You have been arguing that the company is being seriously harmed by theory Y adherents and dangerous T-groups which people are being coerced to attend.
> B: Well, yes, maybe I do have some questions.

(c) Confronting by asking individual to examine own role in situation.

> A: This self-analytical process creates issues that are not there. [The other day] I made an innocent remark, and E read all sorts of things into it that were wrong.
> INT.: I agree with you. Perhaps another way to confront

E would be to ask him more about his views that led him to make the assumptions that you felt were false.

(d) Confronting in a competitive, aggressive manner. After several hours of A and B insisting the YB was a dangerous, soft, manipulative, ineffective philosophy, yet presenting no examples to illustrate their point, the interventionist asked directly for them to give examples of individuals (in the group) who had behaved in ways that they felt were "soft."

> B: I'd say the whole company.
> INT.: It is difficult to deal with such an answer. Could you give a specific example? *(more hesitation)*
> INT.: OK fellows, are you going to be soft on these issues? You speak of integrity and courage. Where is it? I cannot be of help, nor you for that matter, if all you do is accuse the company of being ineffective. You said you are ready to talk—OK, I'm taking you at your word.
> A: Let me try it. B and you get me off the hook later on. *(laughter)*
> B: No, I'm closer to the door. *(laughter)*
> C: Would you mind moving over? I want to get closer to the door too. *(laughter)*

After the laughter subsided B gave an example which eventually illustrated that he was partially misperceiving reality because some of his cohorts had purposely withheld information, lest they harm him.

(e) Confronting by expressing own genuine bewilderment. For an hour or so many of the group members seemed to be skirting an issue that the interventionist inferred to be hostility toward the OD group.

> INT.: I need to ask us to stop for a moment. I feel a real sense of bafflement. On the one hand, the OD group seems to be seen as the top executives' "baby"—it has direct

access to it. On the other hand, I sense (gives two examples of statements) that some individuals feel angry about
this. Am I misreading?

F: (a moderate) No, I think you're reading me accurately.
I think many of us feel that the OD group is too close to
the top.

INT.: What do you experience that leads you to describe it
as "too close"?

First, several individuals gave examples where OD
people have evaluated executives and given their private
reports to the top three officers. Second, the executives
rejected a program of T-groups that the OD group had
developed where the line executives who were to attend
had no say about what T-groups they were assigned to.

The interventionist supported these concerns and came
down very hard against such behavior. The discussion led
to a clarification of issues, reduction of fears, and the development of a new policy for the OD function.

SUMMARY

I. Dynamics of client system

A. The interpersonal and group dynamics of the client
system were those typically found in other groups which
did not contain many members who were predisposed to
be competitive. An analysis of individual interaction scores
suggested that the scores tended to be distributed into two
patterns. The adherents of XA behaved competitively,
while the adherents of YB behaved less competitively.

However, the YB adherents did not tend to behave, in
that group, as openly and with as much experimentation
and trust as they did when by themselves. This suggested
individuals were capable of learning to behave in several

different ways and that the forces toward XA were stronger than those toward YB. One reason was that the YB adherents believed that one should not order others to manage by principles closer to YB.

An unintended consequence was to make the YB adherents look (in the eyes of the XA adherents) as if they were weak and could not defend their view. This perception was partially a distortion because the YB adherents could defend some of their views. It was partially based on reality because the YB adherents lacked the cognitive maps that they knew were needed for the management to be more effective, not to mention the task of convincing others.

B. XA adherents tended to polarize and caricature YB in several different ways. They stated that YB:

1. Was not oriented toward getting the job done and making profits.

2. Overemphasized interpersonal processes and feelings. This created the danger of an overexamination of feelings, an unnecessary consequence of opening up Pandora's box with the necessary consequences of runaway feelings, confusion, and disunity.

3. Was soft management because it did not tend to confront excellence of task achievement and develop strong controls over performance.

4. Required adherents to see themselves as weak and needing help, especially in interpersonal activities.

These polarizations have a basis in reality. The proponents could cite examples to illustrate their points. However, they tended to fail to be aware of the even larger number of examples available to illustrate that the same consequences exist in an XA world. For example, many wasted hours in meetings, employee apathy, and non-involvement cost many millions of dollars, reduced profits, and reduced effective action. XA adherents overemphasized their type of process, such as control procedures, formal structures, and job descriptions. XA management does not have an enviable record in confronting incompetence or apathy. Indeed, shrewd employees know how to use the executives' dislike for confronting feelings to maintain their apathy or substandard performance. They know that if their performance is clearly poor (the performance is clearly and validatably below standard) an XA manager will fire them because feelings do not have to be confronted. However, if they maintain a substandard performance that is not clearly below standard (or if it is, it can be attributed to organizational factors), then they will be relatively safe. There is little likelihood of their being confronted, because this would open up all sorts of issues of trust, organizational consistency, and the rewards for innovation and risk taking, as well as the executives' behavior. These process-type issues are precisely the ones the executives do not wish to confront.

C. YB adherents disagreed with the above as representing what they were aspiring toward. However, they would not deny, especially during the transition period, that they would unintentionally create some of the conditions described above. Their view, however, was:

1. YB is action-oriented; it focuses on reducing the barriers to progress by overcoming and reducing the organizational dry rot.

2. Opening up Pandora's box may be bewildering initially; but if coped with effectively, it could reduce the confusion and bewilderment that occur when people behave according to their hidden assumptions about others and their fears and incorrect assumptions about what was in the Pandora's box.

3. Dealing with feelings effectively will create not disunity and confusion, but unity and trust. Ineffective

coping with or refusal to cope with feelings is what creates disunity and confusion. However, given the values against the open admission of these conditions, they are carefully hidden under layers of dry rot that are covered with luminous shiny paint showing loyalty and team spirit.

4. XA may lead to hard-headed management, but it also leads to bloodied subordinates who become punchy and soft.

XA adherents preferred to cope with this intergroup reality (within their own group) by denying it ("We're all on one team," or, "Tell me to be YB and I will"); by insisting on tighter controls ("A leader is the nosecone on the ship"); by setting off repeated alarms of impending danger ("We're not going to achieve our profit objectives"); by behaving in ways that make it difficult for subordinates to discuss their views of the impact of the intergroup phenomenon on the remainder of the organization.

The YB adherents prefer to confront the issues in order to work through the differences and develop a consistent management philosophy. However, they felt at a loss as to how to do this. Their proposed strategy was to bring in an interventionist to assist them.

Bringing in an interventionist, they would say, was an admission that they could not cope with the situation. Moreover, looking back, several had hoped that the interventionist would "take on" the opposition and reduce it. This hope suggested that they were willing to become dependent upon the interventionist and let him do the controlling, directive activity that they felt was necessary.

These feelings were surfaced and discussed. The discussion led to the members becoming even more certain that there was no substitute for their becoming more clear about where they stood. Each began to develop his position paper, which attempted to respond to the thorniest questions with which he was being faced. This led to their beginning to become more consistent, more authoritative about where they wanted to go, and less dependent on the interventionist.

Interestingly, a few weeks later an important crisis occurred. There was a highly emotionally charged confrontation among several of the key adherents to XA. (There were issues of mistrust and miscommunication involved.) The initial reaction of one of the officers was to telephone the interventionist. Two others, however, asked why not deal with this issue by themselves. A series of confrontation meetings were developed and held. The executives were able to confront the issue openly and resolve it. Two of the XA adherents were positively impressed with how they were helped through a process of open confrontation.

II. *Dynamics of intervention*

A. The interventionists began by conceptualizing the problem as overcoming the restraining forces toward valid information, free choice, and internal commitment *(not as overcoming resistance to YB).*

The objective of the confrontation session was to identify the restraining forces being created by *both* sides. Examples of restraining forces toward genuine understanding and cooperation between the subgroups were (1) fear of expression of feeling, (2) making psychological mountains out of irrelevant personal or random events, (3) fear of inaction and waste of time and resources, and (4) coercing people to work on process issues before they were ready.

Thus the interventionists, during the session focused on how both sides minimized the commonalities between their positions, polarized the differences developed information to maintain their views, and became relatively closed to influence by "facts."

The conditions were similar to those of an intergroup rivalry and competition with the objective of someone winning and someone losing.

B. Although an intergroup phenomenon did exist, the interventionists did not deal with the issues in ways recommended in the literature to reduce the intergroup conflict (such as to split the group into subgroups, make separate diagnoses, focus on ways of defining subordinate goals, etc.). There are several reasons:

1. The XA adherents had refused to attend a meeting where their behavior would be examined.

2. The XA and YB adherents agreed that they had common goals. Both wanted to achieve a certain set of financial objectives. The differences lay in the ways of managing the organization so that it could achieve the goals.

3. The XA group denied any intergroup phenomenon. They kept talking of being on one team. They insisted that any view of an intergroup rivalry was an illustration of the distortion that can come by focusing on group processes.

The interventionists, therefore, concluded that to define the session as an intergroup problem would be so threatening to some of the key XA participants that they would resist, become emotional, and soon find themselves precisely in the situation that they wished to avoid. They could then correctly question whether they had been given an opportunity for free choice and internal commitment to such a meeting.

C. Another set of restraining forces toward generating valid information, free choice, and internal commitment were the perceptions the XA adherents held that the interventionists were hired to persuade them to accept YB.

These perceptions had to be corrected if the interventionists were to be effective.

They began the session by stating that they were not present to take sides, nor had they been asked to do so. However, they realized that such words, at best, could be reassuring; at worst, seen as a not too subtle ploy. The most effective way for the interventionists to communicate their position would be to behave as consistently as they could with their view. They confronted all participants' behavior whenever it was ineffective (including their own); they questioned XA assumptions that only YB had difficulties; they surfaced the occasions when YB adherents were being inconsistent; they strove to behave competently under conditions of continual mistrust and pressure. They strove to be authoritative without being authoritarian. They attempted to show that they held a position with as much clarity and with as much openness to having it disconfirmed as they could develop. However, if continually punished and misquoted they, too, could call a halt to those tactics.

D. Apparently the fact that the interventionists could talk rationally and meaningfully about YB-type of processes and could become angry helped to decrease the misperceptions about YB and increase the willingness for further diagnosis and experimentation on the part of the ambivalents and later the XA's.

Much more research is needed to understand the processes involved that led to these consequences. Some hypotheses that might be explored are:

1. As is the case in the field of science, theories are rarely overthrown by empirical evidence. Only a more comprehensive and more accurate theory can overcome a less valid theory. The same is true for management theory. Theory X may be incomplete and, in certain critical areas,

invalid. However, even if this were proven beyond any doubt, the manager would have difficulty in altering his views unless he found another theory that would be able to provide answers to his everyday challenges. One hypothesis, therefore, is that XA adherents can begin to consider YB when they are offered a map that provides some orderly and consistent ways of YB management. We are a long way off from this state of affairs, especially in areas of organizational design, administrative controls, and reward and penalty systems.

2. The interventionists' diagnosis suggested that *both* XA and YB had validity. The task was to define the conditions under which each was more effective.

3. Seeing that there was a solid component of rationality to YB meant to the adherents of XA that they could be effective with the other view.

One of the problems in many organizations is that interventionists' maps are so incomplete and contradictory that they defend themselves by responding to clients' requests for rational maps by stating that they must experience the theory first and then develop their map. In the writer's experience this places the interventionist in the unusual position of either lying or offering the client an opportunity to develop a map which can never be public. How else can the interventionist explain that, after going through many experiences (like T-groups), he has no effective way of communicating to a client about theory?

4. Experiencing interventionists who seem intellectually and emotionally secure in their positions may make it easier for the clients to "give in" and become temporarily, or permanently, dependent on the interventionist. The latter dependence is not functional; the former is functional only if it is temporary. Both need to be surfaced and confronted.

E. The primary activity of confrontation used by the interventionists was the surfacing of dilemmas and inconsistencies. There was little need to evaluate directly or condemn individual views, feelings, and attitudes.

The interventionists, however, did evaluate generalizations made about people and organizations by comparing them with the research literature.

The primary assumption that underlies the strategy is that individuals have a high need for competence and constructive intent. Being faced with an inconsistency that they create therefore creates a tension to examine it in order to learn and to become less inconsistent.

F. The approach of focusing on inconsistencies has the consequences, in addition to resolving the substantive issue, to induce the individual (or group) to ask, "Why am I inconsistent?" This, in turn, may lead the members to examine personal or group processes which may help the clients to become more aware of the extent to which they are the origin (an important cause) of some of the problems in their organizations.

Chapter four

Organization C

Case study C focuses on the top-management group (TMG) of a very large corporation. The president (P) and all the officers had undergone some form of laboratory education. The corporation had a relatively large and very competent OD group designing and managing the organization's development program. In several cases below, I will raise some questions about their strategy and activities. These questions are relatively easy to ask with hindsight. Those who have been on the firing line can empathize with how often (by looking backwards) one can think of several more effective ways to behave. This is especially true for those who are interventionists. First, they are in a position of continual stress. Second, the state of tested knowledge is so primitive that the interventionist is expected to accomplish a job, at least as difficult as reaching the moon with a practically nonexistent tested technology, with less than adequate funds, and with executives whose attitudes range from ambivalence to doubting if the trip is necessary.

The high interest in OD and theory Y management was generated about five years ago when, after careful analysis, it was concluded that in the past, under dominating leadership, the corporation had suffered in terms of generating innovating ideas and developing and keeping younger executive talent.

The incumbent president, himself a product of the history of the organization, committed himself to explore changes in structure and climate in order to bring it back to the world leadership position it had maintained for many years.

The client's perception of the problem

After several years of concentrated OD effort the TMG was formed to deal with long-range organizational problems. Progress began to occur especially in the effectiveness of problem solving. The president and the OD professionals were able to relate some initial major changes in the organization to the OD program.

Recently, however, the TMG felt that they had reached a plateau in their effectiveness. Moreover, several internal studies suggested a beginning sense of disenchantment at the lower levels with the lack of progress of the OD programs. One such study was a recent organization-wide experiment which had been held, where all of the managers and executives were asked to develop the future goals of the organization. They met in small groups and fed their reports up to the department heads. These reports, in turn, were collated and given to the TMG. One of the nine most important categories of data obtained from this exercise was called "leadership issues." According to the organization's own analysis, "The most prominent (issue) was a feeling of lack of leadership from the top of the company." They were getting mixed signals from the top about application of OD principles to current company practices. Does the organization really mean to genuinely involve managers at all levels in problem solving?

Another source of data came from the follow-up conferences to a series of short laboratories plus a special OD survey on the progress of OD programs (with twenty-six managers, five from TMG; six department heads; and nine other managers chosen randomly). The results of the data were organized around the categories developed from the study described above. The second study concluded that ". . . dissonance is being experienced between OD principles and what is actually happening in the organization." The feedback from the short labs included the following conclusions: (1) There was uncertainty about management commitment to new ways of managing; and (2) openness and collaboration are highly valued but they are not being practiced generally.

In another section of the analysis it was noted that the lowest levels of management felt that most progress had been made. TMG members were intermediate and the department heads least positive.

Finally the top six OD professionals attended a meeting about the present state of the company OD program. They agreed unanimously with the conclusion that "P has not been able to convince others in management that he really meant organizational change."

The TMG concluded that, in order to make the OD program more effective, they would have to examine their own behavior. They believed that if they could not alter their behavior, then it would be impractical, if not unfair, to ask other groups at the lower levels to become more effective. This did not mean that they would not encourage educational programs at all levels. It meant that they accepted their primary responsibility for setting the climate in the organization about OD.

It is interesting to note that unlike the previous two top-management groups, this one did not hesitate to own up to its responsibilities for some of the reduction in the rate of progress. The interventionist was, therefore, asked to make a diagnosis of the interpersonal and group dynamics of the TMG in order to generate some suggestions as to how the TMG can help itself become even more effective.

The diagnosis of the interpersonal and group dynamics

Three regular top-management meetings dealing with everyday sales, finances, and administrative problems were taped and analyzed by the interventionists in terms of the category scheme described in Chapter 1. The interventionist did not know (and was not told) that all of the members had been to laboratory programs. The results are presented in Table 5.

The results are reminiscent of the competitive executive group in organization A. Conformity to ideas, not helping others, and inconsistent behavior were relatively high. In 655 units of behavior only one instance was noted of someone helping someone else.

The interventionist met with the TMG to give them feedback of his analysis. In addition to discussing the material in Table 5, the interventionist made the following points during his presentation:

TABLE 5   *Scores of Top-Management Group*
(expressed in percent)

	Session I N = 255		Session II N = 200		Session III N = 200	
	N	%	N	%	N	%
Interpersonal:						
Own *i*	190	75	138	69	137	68
Open *i*	50	19	34	17	34	17
Not helping others	15	06	28	14	29	15
Helping others	1	00.4				
Norms:						
Conformity *i*	136	54	101	55	102	56
Concern *i*	106	41	98	44	97	44
Individuality *i*	11	05				
Antagonism *i*	2 less	01	1 less	01	1 less	01
Inconsistent behavior:						
Own *i*—Conformity *i*	83	33	78	39	80	40

1. The group climate is strongly influenced by competitive behavior. When important points are made, they tend to be made in a "selling" manner.

Examples of selling are:

"The *real* problem facing us is. . . ."

"What you are *really* saying is. . . ."

"The nub of the problem is clear. . . ."

"You can't fail if we. . . ."

"The very basic issue is. . . ."

"You've got to. . . ."

"Let's face it, if we would only. . . ."

2. "Selling" and "persuading" tend to:

(a) Make the "seller" feel he is being articulate and powerful.

(b) Reduce the probabilities that the "customer" will buy because the customer senses that the emotional component is stronger than the rational, yet the speaker is insisting that he is being rational and asking others to be the same ("Let's look at the facts"). Under these conditions, the listener may mistrust the "sales pitch." He may see it more as the speaker trying to win him over to protect his department interests than to help create a climate where the optimal decision is made.

Under these conditions the potential customer tends to immunize himself from being infected by the enthusiasm of the seller by turning him off; not listening, but preparing his own sales pitch; and if he does listen, it may be to find the weaknesses in the other's position. Any of these reactions would lead the original seller to feel less effective. His reaction would then tend to be to increase his selling and to feel that the other person is somewhat stubborn or defending his "narrow departmental view." Thus there is a recycling which tends to increase the selling and competitiveness.

3. Under these conditions

(a) Individuals will *not* tend to feel they are heard and understood.

(b) The time available to be "on the air" will tend to be scarce, so once one has the floor, one would give his speech that includes rebuttal as well as any other comments that one has been trying to say or has been thinking. One diplomatic way to do this is to "relate" these nonrelatable items to the previous comments. For example, one may say, "I agree with Bill, and I should like to add a few more points," or "I agree with Joe, however" (and then disagree).

4. There will be very little helping one another to own up to, be open to, and experiment with new ideas. The pre-

dominant stance will be one of the individual contributors competing with each other to be heard.

The result will tend to be a group discussion that does not seem additive. Individuals will report that other members do not speak to the point, or they tend to speak simply to be heard or to protect their departmental positions.

5. All this could tend to lead to feelings that group meetings are a waste of time, and what is needed is a good strong leader.

Three members did state these views toward the end of the meeting. One asked, in a voice that led the observer to infer that he was asking, "What the hell did we accomplish today?" Another followed (a softer, but perhaps equally disappointed voice), "Not a damn thing."

A lively and very involving discussion ensued about the interventionist's comments. The interventionist began to note among the members a sense of openness, an ability to take risks and to show trust that he had not heard on any of the tapes. Here was something baffling. A group that had the scores depicted in Table 5 should not behave this competently. The results were violating the expectations of the theory.

The interventionist reported his bafflement to the group members. He was then told that all the members had attended some form of laboratory education. He then asked why they did not behave as effectively during their regular meetings. The members responded that they were not certain and hoped that the interventionist would help them to find the answer to the question.

They believed that his presence did help them to behave more effectively during the feedback session. First, they felt that he symbolized and legitimized the climate of openness and experimentation that they remembered during their respective laboratory experiences. Second, they felt that he was competent and facilitated bringing out their "suppressed" competence.

Evidence for the latter inference was obtained by the analysis of a tape recording discussing their reactions to the interventionist. It was made without the interventionist present and without the expectation that he would listen to the tape recording (permission was granted three months later). All of the clients made positive comments. Nearly half of the transcription is presented below:

P: How does the group feel as to whether that session helped us move along to a more productive discussion here?

A: I had this reaction. I'm going to his report on the previous tapes. He said these things. He said that there was —what he heard on the tapes of our previous meetings— no real listening, that people, to some extent, were preparing their own statement when somebody else was talking and that, in addition, he found very little additive. That is, somebody said something, and very seldom did anybody come along and genuinely add to it. He also said, in analyzing those tapes, that there were, in a sense, two camps. There was one camp that thought these meetings, TMG, pretty much a waste of time, a lot of wheelspinning, and that P should be stronger; that is, get over all this chitchat, lay out a course, and sail. But that there's another camp that says they're not a waste of time, but they certainly can be better; that this is not a waste of time. With that background I thought the meeting Wednesday night was a lot different. There was a lot more real listening on Wednesday night. I thought there was more additiveness, more support. And that insofar as the two camps are concerned that it's a waste of time, pure guesswork on my part. I would guess the people in that camp felt it was not entirely a waste of time and felt better about that.

B: I have a question for you, P. In your comments you didn't say whether you thought this was a constructive meeting or not. I'm just curious to know from your point of view.

P: I thought it was a constructive meeting, and I thought

it was constructive because we changed some of our habit patterns, that we were listening, that some issues of importance were dealt with, and that, in some respects, we came closer together than we had been. I thought Wednesday night we came closer together than we had been before Wednesday night at these meetings. What did you think?

B: I happen to agree with that last statement. I think this was very true.

E: For me, I'd like to go even further; get him back and involved in another session. And I share your feeling that last Wednesday's session . . . dealt with some tough subjects, tougher than we've dealt with in any of these sessions before. Nevertheless we've been closer knit, and, I thought, more open and honest with exchange, people building on the ideas of others, and so forth. How much of that was the interventionist and his skill as a catalyst, as a trainer, if you like? For myself, I think that a substantial part of it was the interventionist.

P: That reinforces what I saw happen in————, where he involved himself with this group to the point where every other group was envious. He had, I think, a very strong catalyst effect on making meetings move ahead and perhaps to free up and progress.

B: My own feeling about the interventionist is that he had a great deal to do with the success of that meeting. And my own feeling was it was because his questions were so incisive, that in answering them you were afraid to answer other than what you really felt, because you knew, I felt, that he'd know it. *(laughter)* And I think he had a great deal to do with it, through that kind of incisive presentation.

G: I share the feelings. . . .

B: Not to beat a dead horse, but the quality that I thought the interventionist brought consistently to that meeting the other night was one of the things that I did not get enough out of NTL, and that is the importance of the here-and-now. That seemed to me the quality he was bringing to it.

A: I wonder also if the comment that he had about the group's willingness to speak up and express themselves didn't also reflect a kind of readiness on the part of the group. This is not to play down the role that the interventionist played. I had a feeling also that most of us were anxious to get on these subjects. We were a little awkward on how we would do it. I think that must be part of what's reflected in his comments and, I guess, would suggest the desirability of trying a little harder to get past some of those first little barriers, start saying what's on our minds. It's very difficult.

A way has been developed to translate the group data into scores that make comparisons possible of the same group over time and among different groups (Argyris, 1965). In Figure 1, two sets of data are presented. On the right-hand side of the graph are the scores of four meetings of the TMG of organization C. The lines above the zero points depict the level reached by positive aspects of the interpersonal and norm scores. The lines below the zero point depict the level reached by negative aspects of the interpersonal and norm scores. Session one of organization C was a regular business session before the feedback session. Session two was the feedback session. Session three represents another regular business session of the TMG after the feedback session and without the interventionist. Session four is a second feedback-discussion session with the interventionist present.

Two points are of special interest. Session two represented the highest group competence and session four the second highest. Sessions one and three were significantly lower. The group seems to have a higher potential for more effective behavior than it manifested when the interventionist was not present.

The second point is that organization C's achievement in sessions two and four compares favorably with another top-management group, which has received, to date, the

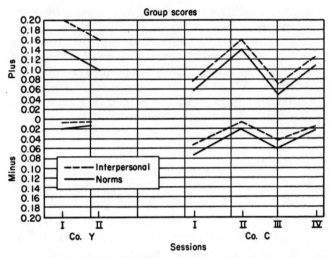

Figure 1. Group Scores of Company C and Company Y

highest scores. (See the two meetings of organization Y on the left-hand side of Figure 1.)

The question arises, why does the group cancel out the potential of its individual members when operating without the interventionist?

An analysis of the reasons for the group's ineffectiveness

In attempting to explain phenomena observed in noncontrived and naturally ongoing settings, it is difficult to specify precise reasons and almost impossible to find the beginning point. Ongoing life is a patterning of complex self-maintaining interrelationships. The most we can hope for, therefore, is to break into the circular processes and identify the ongoing processes thoroughly enough so that we return to our beginning point.

We could, therefore, begin the analysis by noting the

dysfunctional forces that were identified above as existing within the group (the lack of openness, trust, the relatively high conformity, etc.) But let us assume that these are the factors that we wish to explain. This means we want to take our analytical trip by focusing on other factors, so that when we return, we will be able to understand them. Why do they exist, since these individuals had had what they described as useful learning experiences and have shown the potential to put them into effect?

The importance of competitive, win-lose dynamics in the internal milieu of the organization

The first factor identified is the long-held view in this marketing-sales-oriented organization that the most effective behavior is competitive, selling, persuading behavior. The good men win much more often than they lose, and they win on the important issues. The result, therefore, has been to develop institutional rewards, such as promotions, large salary increases, and assignments to challenging task forces to mirror these organizational values.

> B: I do feel that there is competitiveness in this organization. I do think there is a competition that not only exists, but that it has been engendered.
> A: To influence the rest of us? . . .
> B: Exactly.
> C: Sure.
> E: Is it the group that engenders it, or is it P?
> A: Both.
> D: Are we trying to influence or play up to the group or to. . . . I say both!
> P: You know, I find myself competing at a cocktail party with people I don't really care about and that I will never see again.

B: I do too.

G: That's right.

A: Why do we do it?

P: Why do you want to beat someone at poker?

INT.: Could you imagine the day when three vice-presidents competing for scarce financial resources could jointly decide how to share the resources and then recommend it to ——— ?

B: Never!

A: No.

B: Maybe it could happen.

F: Sure, I can understand that—think that we could practice it.

A: Do you *(to P)* think that will become a reality?

P: I don't foresee such a thing. I almost question if it is desirable.

INT.: Why?

P: I think that the requirement to bring a new product to fruition is such a tough process, that it requires such fierce determination, that I cannot see the individual suddenly cooly calculate that the other team has a better deal and the company should give them more of its resources.

C: You can't be objective in that situation.

P: You have to be almost a passionate advocate.

B: P, how can you fit your desire for all of us to participate in defining future company goals and plans into what you just said?

D: Before you answer, I think that I would be willing to give up my two million to someone who we all agree has a better chance of making more money for the company.

P: You had an interesting hedge phrase, "we all agree has a better chance." I've never known that condition to exist.

INT.: Why must this type of competition be here?

P: I don't really know if it must. I know it *is* here. I'm not sure which comes first.

INT.: We may also hear people who enjoy competitiveness.

P: Oh sure, my interpretation of virtually all the men at this table is that they are fairly competitive.

A: *Very* competitive, not fairly.

INT.: Perhaps this is another reason why individuals feel they must behave "correctly" or not at all [also develop unrealistic aspirations].

A second interrelated factor is the time and work pressures under which these executives work. During the few meetings scored, there were forty-one references to pressures. The participants identified role overload and job pressure (in the sense of pressures caused by others) as two critical qualities of life in this organization. The importance of overload and pressure have been documented by Kahn et al. (1964). The lack of time, the induced pressures, and the high overload become magnified under conditions of competitiveness which, in turn, feeds back to make people more competitive because they aspire to win and not to lose.

Under these conditions, it would be difficult for executives to find that time that they would need to practice their newly acquired skills and to deepen and broaden their knowledge in interpersonal and group effectiveness. Getting the job done becomes the primary task.

Lack of knowledge about how to generate the conditions for valid information between individuals

Many of the executives reported that they would be unable to transplant the genuine, experiential, learning-oriented climate back home, even if they had more time and were under less pressure. When pressed for explanations, they were unable to give any, except some strongly held feelings and memories that, "My T-group was a deeply gratifying experience. We were really close," or, "I guess you just have to experience it to understand."

Further interviewing and analyzing of the tapes suggested a possible explanation. The individuals were never taught skills and knowledge in giving and receiving valid information, especially under conditions of getting tasks accomplished. If one analyzes the tapes of the TMG, one finds that most of the feedback that they gave each other was evaluative; attributive, at times; punishing, at times, and producing double binds. To be sure, the competitiveness and pressures could coerce people to behave in these ways. However, there were three reasons to question that those variables provided a complete explanation. First, TMG was the top group in the organization. They could, if they wished, take the initiative to reduce the competitiveness and pressures during their group meetings. Second, many of the members reported that the reduction of competitiveness was one of the outcomes that they hoped would occur as a result of everyone having had meaningful T-group experiences. Third, during training sessions with the interventionist there was little need for competitiveness. Fourth, the men admitted that they had little or no valid knowledge, no map, no set of skills of how to give and receive valid information. For example, only a few had heard of giving information in minimally attributive, minimally evaluative ways. Fewer yet had learned the distinction between feedback that was directly verifiable and feedback that was only indirectly verifiable. Some spoke admiringly of their trainers who had the capacity to say things in ways that produced minimal defensiveness. Others insisted that they remembered their trainers because they were fearlessly open (tell it as it is). Few executives spoke of learning the skills of making explicit and keeping track of the group's history, of helping to make a discussion additive, of helping to create and test for consensus. Many of them had never even had a lecture on these concepts.

Unfortunately data did not exist about what actually went on in the different T-groups that these executives attended. Nor was there any systematic evaluation, by others, of the degree of learning that these men achieved during their T-group experiences. We did have, however, two bits of evidence. First, they viewed their experiences in T-groups as important and meaningful. More compelling, however, was what happened during the feedback session. The quantitative data and the impressions of the interventionist indicated that the group had very high potential to create more authentic relationships and more effective group processes while operating with an interventionist who they respected and who symbolized the values of their T-group.

One possible hypothesis, therefore, is that all the executives are still dependent upon some experts for their effectiveness. This would not necessarily be difficult to understand. It is difficult to generate a *transferable* and increased interpersonal competence as a result of a one-week educational experience.

However, there is the other hypothesis that the individuals were not taught the skills and knowledge necessary to be more effective and to develop more effective groups. There are few laboratories designed by the NTL Institute for Applied Behavioral Science which focus on giving knowledge and generating skills in such areas as giving and receiving valid information or in developing effective group functioning. One or two sessions may be offered during the week. However, these skills cannot be learned in a week or even several weeks. Recently, the writer scored the tapes of several T-groups of two alumni laboratories held by NTL. The majority of the feedback was evaluative and attributive. There was much time spent on analyzing each other of the kind that tends to produce defensiveness, "You are defensive," or, "Could the *real* reason be? . . ."

The data in organization B and in organization C raise some serious questions that designers of future laboratories may find helpful to keep in mind. Alumni may be created who have positive emotional experiences, who truly feel unfrozen, and who experience aspects of themselves never before experienced, but who have not been offered experiences and maps to organize this learning into meaningful guides when they leave the learning situation, nor opportunities to practice these skills necessary to become more competent interpersonally.

But, one may respond, we cannot accomplish everything in one week. Is it not better to give individuals a sample of an authentic experience than to worry about developing competence? They can develop competence later. One answer is that those who come back do not seem to develop such competence. Another is that many of the present alumni laboratories are not designed to develop interpersonal competence and relate it to organizational effectiveness. One reason that the alumni laboratories are not designed to develop interpersonal competence may be that the alumni who return are those who return for another emotional experience. They tend to see the attempts to help them conceptualize their learning or practice theory skills as "mechanistic."

This leads to a more important question. People who equate the development of maps and skills as mechanistic and the emotional experience as organic have split the intellectual from the emotional. Is this split valid? T-groups were begun precisely because the split did not make sense (only, in those days the cognitive maps were seen as more important). Could it be that laboratories have developed in such a way that they are reinforcing the very problem they had been originally designed to overcome? If so, what goes on in laboratories that leads the participants to value the emotional aspects at the expense of the intellectual? These questions require early research attention because the behavioral scientists involved in designing new learning experiences could be creating their own set of negative unintended consequences.

Low confidence in selves and in own group

There is another reason why the dependence for further learning on successive T-group experiences may unintentionally cause some difficulties. The difficulties were observed in TMG. Given the low openness, low trust, low ability to develop an additive discussion, some of the individual members began to *lose confidence in themselves and in their group.* They began to doubt if they could be as effective as they had been in their T-group and to doubt the potential of the TMG. The decrease in confidence in self and in their group tended to increase the probabilities that the members would fall back on their previous styles; and so we obtained the patterns described at the outset in the first three sessions.

Some excerpts from two meetings which were held to discuss these issues with the group are presented below. Although the material is anecdotal, the reader is asked to keep in mind that the excerpts presented below represent a consensus. The interventionist continually tested to ascertain the degree to which the group as a whole agreed with the diagnoses made by certain subgroups.

> A: *(to P)* I thought I was sore at you and, quite frankly, I was. But, in reflection, I was sore at the group. And this was the point that C and a few others are making. There is no support from the group. I learned afterward that I had individual support. But where were they when I needed them?

E: Yes, that's a good point.

C: This is an important problem. I think that everybody belongs on the list [of not supporting others by being open]. Now that I think of it, there is a lot of discussion about P; but is he our real problem? We all met for two years, without P, and we weren't any more open. It seems to me that there is an unwillingness on the part of people to take a risk, and without that I don't know how trust is ever going to be established. And when there's no trust, there's not going to be any open communication.

E: Yes.

G: That's right. *(Several others nod their heads)*

C: We have worked with each other for a very long time. We've developed likes and dislikes about each other. It's very difficult to get enough initial trust started for people to be open on what they've been closed about for years.

H: I sense this is a problem in this group. And I'm relatively new in this group.

G: Yes, typical of us is when A and B sit there and say, "Isn't it a shame that the group doesn't do that?" Let's say X feels very strongly about it. He returns to the meeting; that very issue comes up and he doesn't say anything about it. Then Y sits there and says nothing. The trust is destroyed.

P: Now that you are saying this, I'll say that there isn't anyone who doesn't act differently with me on a one-to-one basis. If you say that I act differently with you, I've got to say that's right, and you act differently with me when you're with me alone than in the group. *(More discussion on the multiroles of individuals)*

A: I think we're facing a very important issue right now. Are we getting enough for our money out of the TMG? Do we really want to make this group work? Maybe not. Why not face up to it? Is everybody going to sit around and say, "Yes sir, boy, I want this thing to work."

B: I think all of us feel this is a good idea. None of us is skillful enough to really make it work. We get into these meetings, and all of us, including P, try to practice [at being more participative], but we're not very good at it.

C: When I think of taking a risk, I have to ask myself, "What

is the purpose? What's the value? What's the payoff?"
I see no payoff in this group for taking a risk.

D: I see no support.

E: Maybe in this group self-interest comes first. The group
comes second. I don't think this is anything to be ashamed
of. I feel no responsibility to the group.

INT.: Does this not mean that there might not be very much
concern about the effectiveness of this group as a whole?
If so, I do not know of any skills that are genuine that
will help overcome the lack of commitment.

A: Yes.

INT.: This could also feed back to make P more anxious
about the members' commitment to this group.

G: TMG is supposed to be a learning experience. But little
of it is going on. No one is learning from anyone else. Few
people are leaving meetings having learned how to be more
effective.

C: Still we mustn't forget we've come a long way from where
we were.
[Yes . . . yes! *(cite several examples of progress in long-
range planning and budgeting)*]

The feelings of low confidence in selves, in others, and
in groups can easily act to negate, in the eyes of the executives, the important progress made. If it continues, it can
raise genuine doubts in people's minds even though their
progress (in comparison with other groups) may be quite
rapid. In other words, the individuals may develop unrealistic levels of aspiration which, in turn, increase the
probabilities of failure, and the cycle is closed.

An example of the doubts raised:

A: Do you think we might be kidding ourselves? Maybe
we're getting a little more sophisticated as a group in
game playing. We are sitting here lulling ourselves into a
false sense of security that we are making progress, when
really progress is not there.
*(Interventionist should have let or asked the group mem-
bers to answer the question first.)*

INT.: A possibility is that progress is being made. With increased openness people are able to see new horizons for openness.

A: Are you trying to make friends with us?

INT.: Let's talk about that. One of the binds that I experience in this group is that if I say something positive about the group I might be mistrusted.

C: I think that we would tend to mistrust positive statements from you or anyone else.

An illustration of the unrealistic aspirations that can develop under the conditions was:

D: Let me ask a question. It relates to the atmosphere. I get the feeling that we're looking for 100 percent success. Mistakes are not permissible. There we have to work on a perfect system. There doesn't seem to be room for error. Does anyone else have that feeling?

E: I do.

C: We do that for this group, for the new products, for everything.

A: I don't have the impression we are striving for perfection.

B: Maybe if we can set a level of aspiration to which we all agree. . . .

Feelings of failure and nonauthenticity

When the executives began to compare their behavior in the back-home situation to their behavior in their T-group, they saw a large discrepancy. Since they were, organizationally speaking, the top group, it was difficult to blame their failure on others (although as we shall see some of it was attributed to their leader).

To the *more* committed there was also the sense of failure that came from knowing that one was not behaving as authentically as one wished. As a result, the individual began to question the applicability of authenticity, or he withdrew from the group, or he reverted to his old style of behavior, or some combination of these adaptive mechanisms. The *less* committed had their questions and fears confirmed. They remain less committed.

Dependence upon the president

The president of this organization was committed to giving the experiment a genuine chance to succeed. He worked very hard to make it succeed, even though, at times, his behavior was temporarily a barrier to progress. To his credit, whenever he was aware of this he invited feedback, so that he could correct it.

As members' confidence in the group and themselves decreased, P became more anxious. He wanted to do everything he could to help the members increase their confidence. Sometimes his attempts were effective, and sometimes they were not.

According to the interventionist, the group tended to underestimate P's attempts at openness and magnify the impact of those interventions that were not as effective. They seemed to be less tolerant of his errors and more demanding of him than they were of themselves. Moreover, in the eyes of P (and confirmed by the interventionist), the men were frequently willing to pass the difficult decisions to P. This buckpassing would concern P. He would take on the responsibility, but then become more directive and authoritarian. Such behavior would be seen by the members as evidence that P did not really want to change his behavior. The subordinates used P's defensive behavior as evidence for impunging his motives; whereas their incompetence was seen as evidence of their incompetence and not as evidence to question their motives.

P was aware of his ineffective interventions and continuously asked for feedback. But, what is the probability that P will get useful feedback on his behavior if the group is questioning his motives? The answer is, not very high. For example, as the excerpts below suggest, when they focused on P's behavior, they gave him evaluative and attributive feedback.

Another problem was that P felt he should not confront certain members about their potential dependence on him. He felt that may embarrass the executives. However, such a strategy had the unintended consequence of making it more difficult for the subordinates to confront P and themselves on this issue.

Some illustrative excerpts are:

INT.: So, at times I feel that the group is quite willing to be dependent on me. Maybe we're doing the same thing to P, and of course he reinforces it, at times anyway, by his behavior. Does that make any sense?

A: Sure.

C: I think every group seeks a leader.

D: You're also not only seeking a leader, but also seeking an expert on some specialized function.

P: When we've had discussions, we haven't criticized our meetings. I think our program calls for it, doesn't it F? One of the standards we have that. . . .

G: Usually we have a time bind, though.

E: Right now we have really no time bind, but we don't even have a . . . nothing's happening. I shouldn't say nothing, but you know what I mean.

INT.: It's difficult. Someone put it beautifully—constipated. *(laughter)*

A: *(to Int.)* One of the things you mentioned at lunch about the possibility of doing was to take examples from tapes and show us well-structured behavior, if you could find any, constructive behavior. Were you planning to do that today? Is that in the schedule?

INT.: No, it wasn't. But I could. I'd prefer to try it another way. Namely, to take a section of the tape, and all of us can listen to it and analyze it. I'd add my two cents, but I'd want other people to add theirs, because it may be that what I saw as not being very effective some people could see as being quite effective.

(During another session)

A: P made a flat statement that we've got a bucket full of new ideas, and our problem is carrying these through to fruition. That's not a statement that's going to encourage disagreement. The context was, goddamn it, let's pay attention to that part of the job. So we did.

B: I didn't make that interpretation at all. I took the statement not as a flat by-God, but that historically our experience about making new ideas pay off has not been good. I did not take P to be closing the door to new ideas.

A: The net effect was that the whole group was asked to devote its attention to topic A rather than B [B being the more important and creative aspects].

C and D: Yes, yes!

B: I'll buy that.

E: I got turned off.

INT.: Is there any way in this group when people feel they're being turned off, they can at least raise the question? Can you not discuss group processes?

F: We agreed we would do it—but we haven't been very successful.

A: That's what I said before. On an issue as crucial as this one we haven't been quite as open as we are on lesser issues.

Another illustration of how the TMG experience of P was obtained occurred during a meeting where P's behavior was discussed. The initiative to discuss P's behavior came from him. The data to which the subordinates refer below came from an organizational diagnosis conducted in the entire organization.

P: I would say, let's discuss my leadership in these terms. What does it mean? What are you talking about? What do you think I can give? Or, what would you like? Would you like me to tell you what you should do? How do you interpret these? These are your divisions, where to begin?

D: One issue that came up quite frequently was the question of the attitude taken toward new ideas and innovations. The climate which is obviously set by the leadership is not always viewed by the organization as a whole as being one that is receptive to new ideas. "Gee, this is the way we've done it, why do we want to do that?"

P: Why don't we discuss that then? What do you think my reaction is to new ideas or innovated proposals? Do you feel I impose a climate? How, one way or the other? Anybody care to comment?

B: I guess some doubt has been generated about your stifling. *(laughter)*

C: Are there any good comments? *(laughter, mixed voices)*

E: I feel we must continue.

F: Really?

A: Quit while you're ahead!

C: What I'm saying, P, is some people might not feel the complete freedom to come forth with something like this because, by God, you'd better not say it to P unless you can back it up 1, 2, 3 down the line, this way.

P: I think that's prejudgment on their part. Unless we're having a cup of coffee after a golf game or something. But If you're talking about the action-decision meetings we have here, I think that's a good observation, and I could say it was accurate. I don't think they are meant to be a kind of happy little forum where we sit around and talk out ideas. What I'm saying is, I like new ideas but, my God, for every 100 new ideas there's only one of them that ever reaches test marketing because a lot that are labeled new ideas are not necessarily good. By the time they get here I like them; I like them, but I also like them good. New isn't enough. A new bum idea is a lot of expense, no profit.

D: Maybe your answer is "no." There has not been a reluctance down the line to really evaluate things which may be good. . . .

G: You have to ask down the line, I think.

D: I was saying if there is such a reluctance, it may trace to a belief that P is not receptive.

E: It sounds like you're saying, "P, you don't want to hear the idea until it has been tested." Am I correct?

P: I don't want an idea proposed, and I don't want an idea delivered to me to work on. "Hey, P, I got a good idea for you! Now you take it and see if you can make it fly."

B: There was one comment that came out of my group that I think at least represented the thinking on this, whether it's correct in the judgment standpoint or not. The comment was on our managerial approach, and when they're talking about a managerial approach they're talking about P, let's face it, the top. The risk taking seems to position many of our efforts as defensive moves within the existing framework of our business. Now at the time that was said we had a long discussion on what their ideas of a defensive move were, and they look on (the product) as a defensive move, not some action that is short term in the market place that you would think of as a defensive action. They're looking at (the product) as a defensive action to take away business from an existing category where somebody else is in there, with not an identical product, but a product that. . . .

P: I think we were the first ones on the market in the United States with. . . .

The leader was aware of his frustrations and difficulties with the group. For example, the interventionist helped the group to become aware of how they attempted to push the "nasty" decisions onto the president. He then commented:

P: I've got to tell you, you put it in terms of reducing my anxiety. Lord knows that may be right. But it's not the way I perceive it. I see it as the group having spent some time saying, "Look what's happening around here. These new product development guys don't come at the right time to our division to seek our advice. This has been as bothersome as hell to us." And so you say, "We'll set about seeking what these inputs are and how the organization should go about getting them." And I see that as a reasonable objective and something, in a sense, that the group has asked for and not a satisfaction of my anxieties. I have anxieties, but that isn't really high on the list. That was my motivation as far as I know.

INT.: No, I didn't understand, but maybe others did. Did you?

C: . . . personally, I got exactly what you said—that P had decided he was going to have this and we rebutted. The discussion went on for two hours and then finally came back to what P wanted. So I think you're right.

INT.: But why did others of you—I still didn't understand what reason you feel you had to stick to a discussion P wanted and not to one that you people thought was the more important problem?

B: I assumed, reading between the lines, that P felt that a (particular) policy would help to utilize our "resources." We didn't think so, unless there was a basic reorganization. P wanted us to get out a policy guide; we wanted a basic reorganization.

INT.: OK. That might mean that P is saying, "Let's not talk about issues that might cost more money at this point, or bring in new people, or change things. Let's first straighten out the resources, realization of the resources we now have." So I can see him as responding to what concerns him, which I think this group reinforces when it said to him, "OK, can we spend more money?" And he finally said—had to say—"No, damn it, we can't!"

F: Well if we want to be open, why don't we ask P? Was that one of your motives?

P: I think it was. All during the discussion they kept saying, "Now can we reorganize the company?" That was, you know, exasperating to me, because we'll reorganize the company, and we still won't have new products. Yeah, I was partially afraid we'd have a whole program for great reorganization of the company on some basis, and then when we get all through, we still don't use our resources.

INT.: That sounds to me like you don't trust this group to do something that will lead to success for this company, that they'll be willing to intellectually generalize way up

here, reorganize, reorganize, reorganize, and not get anything done.

A: As I viewed the interchange at that time, there were a lot
of hidden agendas. And I think the way I looked at it was
that it was a question of priorities. In several earlier meetings P had made the point, which had gone with no dissent
at that point, that hell, our problem is that we had stum-
bled on several new products at that time. The number of
successful new products could probably be counted on the
fingers of two hands, maybe one. Therefore, the priority
at this point is how can we do what we're already embarked on better and utilize all the resources that over a
long period of time people have said haven't been utilized.

Later on in the discussion the interventionist asked the
group why they felt they had to ask P if there were funds
available.

INT.: Why is it that P had to say that there was no new
money for the project?

A: This is how we have always operated. We try to get as
much money out of him as we can, and he tries to give
out as little as he can.

B: Who else is supposed to tell us that there isn't any more
money?

C: Perhaps [the interventionist] is asking if we really agreed
on the new budget levels, and we agreed to the expense
levels, then why ask P for new funds? We know there
aren't any.

INT.: Yes, this is the question I am asking. I am also wondering if P doesn't feel a bit trapped. TMG members want him
to create conditions for genuine sharing of certain decisions, yet once they are made, some group members still
hold him responsible.

P: *(nods positively)* Yes, I do feel that.

Finally, the excerpt below suggested that the executives
were aware that they may be having a negative impact on
the organization below them.

P: I think that we are responsible for giving the organization mixed signals. We'll have much to go through to learn how to work together better.

A: Sometimes I find that I reflect an attitude of hostility toward a new idea, especially if something is shoddy. This apparently results in people saying that I don't like new ideas.

B: I think that we're all guilty of that. I know that I am certainly guilty of taking a shooting-down approach to some of my fellows who come to me with a half-assed proposal. I have a tendency to run a short fuse on those things.

D: I can plead guilty to stifling other people.

E: I think another failing that many of us are probably guilty of is either an apparent or actual lack of consistency.

Lack of awareness of the difficulties in transition

Another factor that helped to make the transition more difficult was the lack of awareness of how lengthy, complex, and painful the transition processes would be. All of the executives expected to have difficulties during the transition period. None were "true believers" who believed that change would come about if time and good intentions were permitted to combine. However, they did not have an idea of how difficult it would be for them to alter their behavior back at home and to develop an effective group.

For example:

F: I'm not happy with this meeting. We seem to beat everything to death. This is painful, and I think we should re-examine our operation.

A: I'm sorry, but I disagree with F. We are trying to develop a new form of management. This is an experiment. It is new, and we won't be perfect. Rather than saying we're lousy, I think I am learning.

P: We're talking about our style, which is painful. It's not entirely without pain to me—I know it causes you even

more pain. But here we are. The other system of management has not led to any solutions of the important problems. In some ways, I should be the one who'd most relish
the old style. I'll tell you what though, the old style didn't
work then nor would it work now.

Part of the problem may be that the laboratory programs
did not focus adequately on the problems of transition. For
example, of the seven executives asked, none said they were
given even a crude estimate of how long it might take to
make back-home groups more effective. (In the writer's
experience three years, assuming one day a month of ongoing educational activity, is an optimistic time period.)

But more importantly, how could they expect to have
success if they had not developed the knowledge and the
skills basic to the interpersonal and group success that
they wanted?

YB is soft management

Another interesting consequence was that the view that
equates YB with "soft" management began to develop,
especially among the less committed members. Why did
this occur?

If executives attend a laboratory experience and (1)
learn that directive and controlling leadership is ineffective, and if (2) they do *not* learn what is effective, and if
(3) they do *not* learn how to behave more effectively, then
does it not make sense for them to infer that what *is* effective leadership is to be less directive and less controlling? If so, and if they have not learned how to alter their
degree of control by encouraging others to enlarge theirs,
then would it not make sense for them to assume that they
should reduce their control and reduce their activity in task
issues? Indeed, would this strategy not be supported by

the fact that when they attempted to become more active they became more unilaterally controlling and dominating? Would not withdrawal, therefore, be a likely adaptive mechanism, especially if one tells others that he has returned from an experience where he has learned about the difficulties of unilateral control? In short, the very nature of the education that these men received, the incompleteness of the learning, may have led to consequences whose end result would be to stimulate views that equate YB with "soft management." To be sure, at least 40 percent of the eighteen executives in TMG did *not* equate YB with "soft management," but how long will they be able to maintain these views in the context of competitiveness, overload, pressure, and group and individual ineffectiveness?

Transferring dependence onto the interventionist

Another way to cope with the difficulties above was to expect that the interventionist, if skillfull, would as one said, "help us by taking hold of us and showing us the way." The group initially hoped that he could represent the loss created by not having their respective T-group leaders with them.

Indirect evidence for this came after a particular meeting with the interventionist. The reader may recall that session four was the feedback session. It was characterized by a relatively high degree of openness and trust. However, the session was one whose structure was the responsibility of the interventionist (he presented the feedback), and the content focused primarily on analyzing the problems of the group. Given what we now know, it is a plausible hypothesis that the competence that was manifested was partially due to the fact that the interventionist was responsible for the content and that the content focused on diagnosing the group's effectiveness (an issue about which there were understandably many pent-up feelings).

After the "successful" meeting, another one was scheduled. Unlike the previous meeting, no agenda was defined. During the meeting some members began to focus on "next steps" and "becoming more effective." The interventionist took on a more passive role. The group reverted to their traditional pattern. It was, in the eyes of many members, a disappointing meeting. Several weeks later a discussion was held, without the interventionist present, to discuss whether he should be invited again, and the disappointment about the meeting came out.

The following discussion was held:

P: Should we continue with the interventionist?

A: Well, from our previous discussions there are a few things that he pointed out that we didn't get to in the last meeting.

B: Was that because we couldn't get to them or we didn't want to?

A: I don't know.

D: I had a feeling that we were playing games with him and ourselves. A lot of time during that meeting was spent spinning our wheels.

E: I think that's part of the frustration that he was experiencing, too, and reflecting on when he was asking a question, "Do you really want me to work with you? . . ." looking for some sense of conviction that, yes, we did want him there to comment on the process.

D: We certainly weren't working with him, that was for sure.

E: I don't think he was complaining about that; I think he was complaining that we weren't working with each other. He wasn't worried about whether we were working. . . .

H: We weren't helping him help ourselves. *(mixed voices)*

B: But the problem was how can we work with each other? That's much more important.

P: When you say we were playing games with him, what

does that mean? That we were not leveling with him? That we were holding back? What do you mean by that?

D: Well, one example that I can remember was he had mentioned more than once in the two meetings about this dual-hat situation that he kept overhearing you being needled about, and so forth. Well, now at the meeting the other night, 50 percent of the people in the room knew that this problem was solved by two changes. The other 50 percent in the room didn't know this had been done. And every time he brought it up, everybody kept just kind of pounding him down over the head, and so forth. That was an example of what. . . .

E: . . . would do him the courtesy of saying, "Well, that's a subject we're not going to talk about. Let's talk about something else." We just let him try to fish, and he was fishing for the better part of an hour on that . . . and nobody would level with him and say, "We don't want to talk about it or anything else." *(interruption)* and then he got on some of the other topics, kept trying to draw us out. . . .

P: I think the interventionist in the last session invoking his homework and some of the things that happened at the session challenged people on saying, "Boy, when that was done two weeks ago I wasn't really with that." He would come back and say, "Why didn't you say that at the time?" And that's when a veil of silence came down.

A: Isn't that one of the things you're referring to?

B: I don't recall what it was, but A and I were having an exchange on some things, and he kept trying to draw out the whole group and get some more comments on whatever the topic was. Do you remember what it was? It was a topic in which we went back and forth, and he kept trying to draw out everybody and get something on, so that it ended up where it was, batting the ball back and forth across the net between A and myself. And I gave up on it, and I guess A did; finally, the thing kind of went flat. There was apparently no interest on the part of the group either in pursuing the subject or in trying to give the interventionist the satisfaction of either finishing it or burying it. We just kind of left it running on forever.

F: I think, picking up on what B said, there were several

instances in which the question came up as to why some
of us were turned off or in disagreement with something
that you said, P, or there wasn't a dealing with the issue
at that point in time. Why turn it off rather than confront?
And a series of questions at different points in the even-
ing with regard to the relationships dealt with each other,
situations of that type.

G: Yeah, I remember that.

A: But we felt we were playing games with him rather than
ourselves. *(mixed voices)*

C: Sure, we're playing games with ourselves and also playing . . . as a result of playing games with him, but not
deliberately playing games.

B: The interpretation I had was that we were just playing
games with him, not with ourselves.

P: Relate this to where we go from here. As a consequence
do you think we ought to abandon our . . . cut off with
the interventionist at this point? Or should we continue
to send him the tapes occasionally meeting with him?

A: I think he could be very helpful to us.

B: I was one of the ones who originally was very keen about
having a process observer in, and I guess . . . I don't know
how we got around to the tapes. I guess you mentioned
the fact that he had done this type of work for others, and
that it was the feeling that we might have them just to do
the tapes. But I think he can be of help whether he's here
personally or whether he's here in a secondary role, as
listening to the tapes, whether it's the interventionist or
somebody else. I think this interventionist is undoubtedly
good at this, but I think there are other people, if he doesn't
have the time, who could help us. But I'm sure we will
make more progress with him than without him.

F: Or one of his caliber.

P: How do other people feel?

C: I'd like to talk—if you don't mind. I'd like to confess a
feeling that I have, and it is a confession because I don't
think it's a good feeling. At the first meeting with the interventionist, in the hotel, as people have said, he was
prepared and, I felt for myself at least, I was kind of prepared to hear something from him. In other words, he was

a little more to me at that point than a process observer. He had been an analyst because he had listened to a bunch of tapes. And I expected him to and he did help by giving someone else . . . sheets of paper, and so on, that he passed out. When he came the second time, both to lunch and to the recent meeting, I had that same expectation, but it didn't happen. I say I apologize for the feeling because I don't think he should do what I expected him to do. I think the best use of the interventionist, if we want to use him, and I would be one to vote for it, is that he should come, not as an analyst, but truly as a process observer for a meeting at which we try to conduct our business. In other words, instead of reacting to the interventionist, be a process observer and say, "What do you mean by that, A?" And see if he can't build in to our own attitudes about working with each other the kind of responses that we ought to have and seem unwilling to have with each other. Now is that a distinction that's clear? It's clear in my mind. *(mixed voices)*

The predisposition to be dependent upon the interventionist was illustrated in an excerpt from another discussion. Executive A describes his attempts at utilizing questions, only to discover their ineffectiveness when they are not congruent with his motives.

The executives decided that they wanted to continue with the interventionist if he would attend one of their actual working sessions and feel free to interrupt to make process comments anytime that he wished.

A: I listened to you during our first meeting, and I notice that you asked questions. I concluded that it's better to ask questions than to speak persuasively.

INT.: My view of my behavior is that I ask questions primarily when I genuinely want to get information. If I have an opinion I gladly give it. For example, at the beginning, I gave five points about the group.

B: I think that some of us use questions to dodge responsibility for expressing our opinions.

C: Yes, questions are important if they are sincere.

D: Yes, and not if you're trying to get the other guy to fight your battle for you.

F: Or if you're asking a question and the message comes through not silently, but loud and clear that you've already got the answer, and you're setting the other guy up for the kill. *(laughter)*

INT.: Perhaps my questions will also be believed in this light. I'd like to invite anyone to confront me if he infers that I am asking questions insincerely.

A: I don't have that feeling.

B: Neither do I.

F: I think you're an impartial killer. *(laughter)*

In line with the diagnosis above, the interventionist decided to attempt to focus on the here-and-now dynamics of the group. He interrupted when people were being evaluative, attributive, mishearing, etc. He asked the receivers of such behavior to describe their feelings, which were mostly negative. He asked the group members if they had realized that the particular receiver of incompetently given feedback was upset. In all but one case they were not aware, partially because the individual hid his feelings. He asked the giver of the incompetent feedback to experiment with other ways of being more effective.

The executives reacted positively. The meeting was described by many as the best one of the year. "Finally we are learning something that can help us get out of the hole we have dug for ourselves," and "This is what I have been waiting for." These comments are *not* included as any evidence of behavioral change. They are presented to illustrate the hypothesis that the type of learning these executives need most has to do with the basic knowledge and skills related to giving and receiving valid information and developing effective groups.

SUMMARY

Dynamics of client system

The interpersonal and group dynamics were similar to those found in client systems A and B as well as in many other previous competitively oriented executive groups.

Unlike the other executive groups, this one contained members who had had successful laboratory experiences, had presidential support for further learning, and had a skilled OD group to help them continue their learning.

However, their learnings at their respective laboratories may not have been adequate enough to help them transfer their knowledge back home, even though it was to their own group and even though they were the top group in the company. The individual executives, although highly motivated to succeed, had little knowledge and few skills to fulfill their motivation.

The result was a set of complex circular processes that almost guaranteed long-run difficulties. Thus the predominantly anti-individual, competitive, and anti-group effectiveness forces identified at the outset (low openness, low experimenting, high conformity, etc.) were reinforced by the cultural values that rewarded competitiveness and win-lose dynamics (instead of problem solving). These forces were supported, in turn, by the work pressures and job overload. The TMG meetings to increase individual learning were being conducted under difficult conditions.

To continue the processes, many of the individuals had not learned adequately such basic skills as giving valid information and receiving information accurately. This, in turn, led to ineffective group meetings. The ineffectiveness produced a low sense of confidence in the individuals and in the groups. These, in turn, led to feelings of failure and nonauthenticity. The reactions to these feelings were (1) to reinforce the competitive, authoritarian styles; (2) to be dependent on the president (who responded by taking on more responsibility, thereby opening himself for attack as not being genuinely committed to new management philosophy); and (3) to eventually develop the conception of theory Y as soft management. This, in turn, would increase the probabilities that under conditions of work pressure and overload the executives would become even further disillusioned about their group. This, in turn, would increase their dependence upon the original, more unilaterally controlling styles of leadership. And so the cycle is closed; it becomes self-perpetuating and inhibitive of change.

Chapter five

Conclusions I:
Top Management and
Organizational Development

1. The supremacy of pattern A

The three top-management groups manifested the same interpersonal relations, group dynamics, and organizational norms even though they represented (a) three different corporations with very different technologies, products, and external environments; (b) at three significantly different points in time; (c) with three significantly different histories and accomplishments in organizational development activities.

All the management systems were dominated by pattern A (see table on opposite page).

These findings remained consistent almost regardless of the size of the group, the topic being discussed, the conditions of the external environment, the degree of organi-

Behavior tending to be more frequent	*Behavior tending to be less frequent*
Owning up to ideas	Owning up to feelings
Conforming to ideas	Individuality of ideas
Concern for ideas	
Openness to ideas	
Not helping others to express ideas and feelings	Helping others to express ideas
Inconsistent behavior	Consistent behavior

Rarely observed behavior

Experimenting with ideas or feelings
Concern for feelings
Trust of ideas or feelings
Helping others to express their feelings

zational development that had occurred, and the attitudes people held toward individual and group development.

The only major deviation from these findings was observed when a group was under stress. Under stress, groups seemed to magnify their pattern rather than change it. For example competitive, aggressive groups became even more competitive and aggressive.

For the reader interested in individual differences, we report that few seemed to be observed. Different executives tended to behave in the same manner when participating in the group meetings. It is as if the group settings attracted, coerced, or required certain kinds of behavior. The behavioral requirements tended to fit the expectations of the executives because, as we have suggested in Chapter 1, our society programs people with "pyramidal values" which tend to result in pattern A. Executives are especially susceptible to these values.

This does not mean that individuals did not differ along characteristics such as openness, experimenting, etc. It is our hypothesis that they did differ, but one of the consequences of pattern A was to coerce them to suppress many of their differences. For example, many executives were interviewed who reported having strong feelings during the meetings, yet they did not express them because the expression of feelings was viewed as inappropriate. The few who reported they had expressed their feelings seemed, to the observers, to have done so in an intellectualized manner.

2. The predisposition toward personal responsibility is low

Another quality which the overwhelming number of executives who had no laboratory experiences manifested was little predisposition to look "inward" to ascertain the extent to which they might be important causes of the human problems within their system. Their tendency was to place the causes of the problems outside of themselves.

The projection outward was by no means invalid or paranoid. As we have shown, pattern A is coercive, and, therefore, the executives could legitimately maintain that the system was causing their behavior. What the executives seemed to resist doing was to explore the extent to which they were responsible for maintaining pattern A. It did not seem to occur to them that pattern A might be changeable and that as the top executives they could begin to make some of these changes.

Our findings support those of Oshry and Harrison (1966) that executives who have had successful laboratory experiences tend to become more self-responsible. The YB adherents in organization B, for example, were constantly concerned about their personal responsibility and about changing the system. Indeed, as we hope to show below, some of them may have become overresponsible. The majority of the executives in organization C were also aware of the importance of examining their responsibility in a situation or problem. However, they seemed to have great difficulty in creating the interpersonal relations, group dynamics, and organizational norms that are necessary for effective self-examination.

The nature of pattern A provides us with some cues that may help to explain these findings. In a pattern A world little feedback is given the members about their impact upon others and upon their groups; nor are requests for such information sanctioned. One runs the risk of being secretly evaluated as insecure, immature, or queer for asking such questions (Argyris, 1969). I say secretly, because in a pattern A world interpersonal evaluations are rarely shared openly. The result of such relationships is that people have few data from others about themselves. To compound the problem, if they did receive such information, they may not trust it because they know how many times they have held back or distorted feedback in the name of being diplomatic and civilized. It is difficult to trust the feedback from others when you cannot trust your own toward others.

Without valid feedback that can be trusted, self-examination is difficult. The individual is caught between not trusting his own subjective reactions or the reactions of others. How do individuals live with themselves, knowing that they are rarely candid and fearing the same about others? One way may be to suppress the problem and focus on issues outside oneself. Working for years under such conditions, it is understandable how personal causation could become suppressed. The participants will tend to focus on group or organizational characteristics that cause human problems. As we have pointed out in Chapter 1 and elsewhere (Argyris, 1964; 1965), there are plenty of such characteristics.

The difficulty with this strategy is the one that was mentioned regarding the sociologists who prefer to bring about change through structural changes. It assumes that changes at the upper levels are possible by redesigning organizational structures, administrative controls, and so on, without having to change the interpersonal and group relationships. Why this may not be realistic will be discussed in a forthcoming section.

The question to be asked now is, "To what extent is it possible to expect changes toward more valid communication, toward more trust, if people are in systems where the information flow is so censored that they are not able to perceive reality accurately and to behave competently?" As we saw in organization C, many of the executives had not mastered the behavioral skills necessary for competent interpersonal and group relations. Consequently, whenever a good idea for structural change was mentioned, they were unable to deal with it constructively. If the president were to order the change, he realized that he would then be justifiably accused of behaving unilaterally. Moreover, there was ample evidence in companies B and C that executives who accepted orders, but who were not internally committed to the orders, tended to be ineffective in implementing them with their subordinates.

Executives who have participated in implementing changes designed by consulting firms can attest to the difficulties involved. One can even see the resistances and difficulties in the development and introduction of management information systems which fundamentally do not threaten the pyramidal theory X values and, in this sense, should be easier to implement (Argyris, 1970).

3. Lack of valid and useful maps about the transition toward YB

Even if the argument above were not valid, the executives in all three organizations would still maintain that they have difficulty in finding tested designs for new organizational structures, new administrative controls, new reward and penalty schemes, etc. Even if the process toward change did not matter, they would not know what to shoot for. Research is seriously lacking in helping the executive to conceive what a YB world may look like. Since their internal group dynamics were not very effective, they tended not to consider the possibility of using their group to experiment with new innovations. Thus they needed and continuously asked for guideposts. Some lower-level executives, and even some OD specialists, interpreted these requests as conscious or unconscious stalling tactics. In the writer's experience, he could find no evidence for this cynical view.

Nor did the executives ask for complete and perfected designs based on fully validated research. They were quite willing to have incomplete studies that provided examples of the designs toward which they might aspire. They simply wanted some guideposts.

The reason for requesting the information was their high sense of responsibility to their employees and the stockholders. They did not believe it was legitimate to experiment with the lives of lower-level managers or with the administrative functioning of their system without some ideas of the probabilities that they would not harm the individuals or the system. They were taking the position that we hope drug companies take when they produce a new product or that we hope educators take when they produce a new way to teach mathematics. In the latter case, there is evidence to suggest that the absence of internal commitment on the part of the school administrators and teachers may have caused havoc with these programs (Sarason, 1970). Indeed if a cynical view is desired, the one that may be more easily documented is that the lower-level executives and a few OD specialists may be more dependent upon and, therefore, more impatient with the top executives.

4. YB is viewed as leading to soft management

In all three organizations, whether they had just begun to consider an OD program or whether the OD program had existed for five years, the question was continuously raised if YB did not represent soft management. Why was this so?

The XA world emphasizes achieving the goals, with little attention to the human beings, and thus a high cost is paid in terms of the interpersonal and group factors. The executives who tend to be attracted to, become successful in, and are gatekeepers for the new entrants are those whose leadership style tends to be oriented toward getting the job done and ignoring interpersonal issues.

These executives are aware that over the years they may have had to hurt individuals or groups in order to accomplish the tasks. Let us hypothesize that hurting others hurts them, and the way to live with themselves is to find rational reasons for having to be XA. As pointed out in Chapter 1, this is not difficult. XA produces subordinates who are dependent, oriented toward the superior, fear risk taking, and rarely level about interpersonal issues. Under these conditions, XA leadership becomes functional because it is a self-fulfilling prophecy.

To focus on interpersonal and group processes is to ask these men to do something that is not only very difficult, but also something which they have assumed, up until now, would be ineffective. Keeping in mind the time it takes to hold effective discussions on interpersonal and group processes, and given the overload and pressures, most executives report that it is understandable how the executives would become fearful that the organization's goals will not be accomplished.

Moreover, if someone were able to show that it were possible to manage an organization—indeed make it more successful—by focusing on the task *and* the interpersonal and group processes, the executives would then have to face up to the possibility that the truism about the necessity of being "tough" is, at least partially, a self-fulfilling prophecy and potentially could be made into a myth. The potentiality for tough management becoming a myth can be shown by examining the world as it now is and need not wait for the world to become something different. For example, it is intriguing to note that when executives are questioned about YB behavior and softness, their fears and arguments tend to be related to others. Many quickly admit that they would prefer a world that is more open and trusting and shows concern for people. Their fear is that others do not want it so, or that others would accept it in order to reduce their efforts—to "goof off." Concerning the former, if most executives report, when alone, that they prefer YB, then one could argue that the fear that others do not want it is based on lack of information. Why is it that XA executives tend not to test out the possibility that others may feel as they do? Perhaps they do not want to find out the truth. Perhaps they cannot even imagine YB as a valid possibility. Perhaps they do, and when they attempt to explore others' views, their fears about people taking advantage of YB also shine through. If so, would they not tend to attract negative replies? But if people did "goof off," and since these men are the top executives, why can they not confront this behavior? Do they not have the power to do so? What do they fear?

Executives do have the power but, in these three organizations, they disliked using it for such confrontations. Thus XA executives may tend to be soft on confrontation even though they have the power to do so. Why? One reason may be that they know they do not tend to confront effectively. In their experiences confrontations tend to escalate to strong and emotional discussions or, what may be even more devastating, to silence and overt submission.

This possibility is congruent with the findings in the present research literature that employees are increasingly becoming less committed and involved in the organization and are becoming more apathetic, and none of these conditions are being confronted directly by theory X managers. *Thus theory X may be tough on getting the job done; but it is soft on keeping the system healthy, and this softness tends to be covered up.* It is usually left for the next generation to cope with as was the case in client systems B and C. Perhaps this is an explanation as to why some of the world's most productive organizations may also have the world's greatest amount of "dry rot."

If these studies are replicable, then many of the YB adherents are going to have great difficulty in overcoming the dry rot when they return. The educational experiences that these executives were exposed to informed them primarily about the dysfunctional consequences of theory X management. Little time was spent in providing them with ideas and maps as to where to alter their behavior or to redesign their organizations. Even less time was spent in helping the executives begin to alter their behavior. Therefore the executives, as in the case of client system C, returned to a supportive system and were unable to practice much of what they learned and were, therefore, also unable to continue their learning.

Executives who lack the ability to behave congruently with theory Y will not tend to feel very confident in the theory nor in their ability to behave according to pattern B. If they do not feel confident, they will not tend to internalize the theory. If they do not internalize it, the probability is quite high that they will "regress" to their backup style, especially under pressure and crisis. But, this is precisely the moment to which the subordinates may look to test their superiors' commitment to the new theory. Reverting to the more authoritarian behavior by the superior may be seen by the subordinates as proof that their boss is not truly committed. Therefore they may begin to withdraw, which may make the superior more anxious, which, in turn, may increase the probability that he will return to his old style of leadership. Some of these problems were illustrated in our organizations. There were meetings in which people knew that they were not telling everything they knew about a particular issue or problem. Thus they knew that they were being "soft" or ineffective. One possible way was to reduce the dissonance by viewing Y as soft.

Executives who have not been helped to develop new skills will tend to believe that effective behavior is the opposite of the old and ineffective behavior. Thus overcontrolling becomes undercontrolling; overaggression becomes passivity or withdrawal; overrationality becomes overemotionality, etc. Under these exaggerated conditions theory Y would indeed be soft.

The underlying assumptions of theory Y are, for example, the overcontrol by one individual (in these cases the chief executive officer) should be turned into enlarged control by all the relevant individuals (the other top officers), that overrationality be seen for what it is, namely, an emotional response. Rationality includes the expression of feelings when they are relevant to the individual behaving competently and to the problem that one is attempting to solve effectively.

There are three other possible explanations that should be mentioned. Because they are more clinical in nature, they will be more difficult to document or verify.

The first is the one alluded to in organization B, that the executives who worry about YB being soft may be those whose natural style is to be competitive, evaluative, and aggressive. Such a style tends to be inconsistent with YB. If the world became more YB, then they would have difficulty relating to people effectively. They would tend to feel that the culture did not sanction their behavior. They would also run the risk that individuals might see them as deviants and reject them. The result could be interpersonal isolation and failure in those activities that require the cooperation of others.

The second possibility is that the compulsive emphasis on theory Y being soft management could stem from the executive's deeper and perhaps less conscious feelings that his core personality can be soft, that he can be easily overwhelmed with emotions, that he can be genuinely hurt when he finds he must hurt others, and that he therefore can trust neither others nor himself. One way to attempt to cope with these fears is to suppress them, to turn to a complete focus on tasks, to identify with the health of the organization (in order to have "good" reason to be tough on others). Under these conditions describing theory Y as soft management could be a projection. The executive projects his own softness onto a theory of management that seems overidealistic (and, therefore, anxiety producing) and ambiguous (and, therefore, excellent stimulus for projection).

The third possibility is that executives who fear that the expression of feelings "is dangerous," or "could cause a runaway situation," or "could open Pandora's box" may be individuals who have been working hard (but unrealizingly) to keep their own such feelings from coming to the surface. A theory that sanctions the expression of feelings could be a source of anxiety because, if their feelings were expressed, the energy for work might be reduced and the personality softness might surface.

5. YB adherents unintentionally reinforce the concept of soft management

On the other hand, there are several factors that may act, in the eyes of XA adherents, to support their view that YB can be utilized by or lead to individuals being soft about management and change.

First, there is the apparent bind YB adherents are placed in by the very fact that they prefer to provide others with an opportunity for free choice. If the others are XA adherents, they will tend to perceive attempts to get them to change as legitimate *if* the YB adherents are able to present rational, consistent, and empirically validated proof that their system is more effective; *if* they know how to move effectively from XA to YB; and *if* they show competence in using power unilaterally. The difficulty is that the YB adherents will not tend to be able to meet these requirements. Their cognitive maps that describe YB and those that describe how to make the transition effectively are very rough and for many crucial issues (e.g., new kinds of organizational structures and managerial controls) practically nonexistent. The empirical proof that is needed to present evidence of the validity of YB as a management philosophy is just beginning to be generated.

Consequently the YB adherents cannot behave with the degree of certainty that would reduce the anxiety of the XA adherents. Thus the XA adherents may conclude that YB adherents are soft and muddleheaded.

However, and we now come to the second reason, even if they could, the YB adherents would be loathe to use the available knowledge and evidence either to order the changes or to ram them down people's throats. Both strategies violate their philosophy. Their preferred strategy would be to use the information as a basis for the participants to explore the designs and actions that they wish to create for their setting. The information, therefore, would be used less to coerce change and more to provide the foundation necessary for people to explore new ways of managing themselves and taking appropriate risks involved when basic changes are being made.

The third reason is illustrated by what happened in organization B. The YB adherents desired to discuss openly all issues, be they interpersonal or substantive, about which there was disagreement. The XA adherents resisted such discussions with arguments that, "They would take too much time"; "Our job is to produce so and so and not to be a personality factory"; "There are no basic differences"; or finally say, "Look, if you want us to change just tell us exactly what you want us to do and we'll do it."

The YB adherents knew that ordering a YB philosophy of management would be self-defeating, and they knew that the XA adherents couldn't change their behavior that quickly because they (YB adherents) had and continue to have great difficulties in changing theirs.

The YB adherents were also aware of the reality that the

organization had tasks to complete and objectives to achieve, and had to maintain itself. They feared that if too much time was spent on discussion of YB issues, it could harm the output of their system as well as the commitment and effectiveness of several very key executives whom they did not wish to lose. The result was that the YB adherents tended not to push for change but to leave the XA adherents alone.

However, with the passage of time, it became apparent to all the executives that the managers below the top were increasingly frustrated and bewildered with the split at the top about management philosophy. The managers began to complain, at an increasing rate, that the split was causing confusion and divisiveness at the lower levels *and* that the less competent managers were using it to protect themselves against errors they had made but which could easily be blamed on the top-management rifts.

As these complaints increased, the impatience and fears of both YB and XA adherents tended to increase. The YB adherents felt increasingly frustrated. They wanted to confront these issues, but they felt such a confrontation might upset the XA adherents which, in turn, might harm the accomplishment of the organizational objectives. The XA adherents, on the other hand, saw the frustrations and tended to infer that the reason the YB adherents were not taking action was that they were soft.

For example, during a group interview one year after the confrontation session described in Chapter 3, the YB adherents described evidence that some progress had been made in unfreezing the XA adherents. However, the progress was accompanied by increasing frustrations and confusion throughout the organization. Things were getting better *and* worse. The forces of difficulty were overwhelming the forces of progress.

The YB adherents diagnosed their frustrations with the XA adherents as follows:

(a) "They [XA] do not tolerate differences among us [YB]. If we show real disagreements they either become frightened (because the top three should never exhibit publicly their differences) or they ridicule us because we do not seem to know where we are going."

(b) "The XA's abhor and fear conflict among individuals."

(c) "The XA's tenacity with which they maintain the necessity to control and manipulate people is greater than we expected."

(d) "But, what drives us most out of our minds is their tendency to think and problem solve in black and white terms, their lack of ability to deal with abstractions, and, therefore, their intolerance of ambiguity."

These conclusions had led YB adherents to wonder if change would ever come. "Will we ever have a cohesive group, or are we trying to paper over something?" Also, they began to question if they could live with these differences. They were feeling increasingly that they could not. As one of the executives said, "I am not going to be trusting of people who do not value trust. I cannot be open unless the relationship is open. I want to feel some mutual support. I want to feel that if I am being criticized it is because they care for me."

The interventionist asked the YB adherents if they had communicated these feelings to the XA adherents. They responded that they doubted that they had done so clearly. The interventionist suggested that another possibility was that they had not hidden these feelings, that the XA adherents were aware of them, and that would place the YB adherents in the position vis-à-vis the XA's of not being open. If these possibilities were valid, then the XA adherents could question legitimately the YB adherents' commitment to openness and risk taking. In this sense the YB adherents were being soft!

This led one of the YB adherents to say, "You know, I wonder how confronting we really are. When we experience differences, we treat them softly. Once in a while we may get frustrated and come down on them hard." This behavior pointed out another problem; it was not only inconsistent with what they believed in, it also created confusion and ambiguity, something about which they had said the XA adherents were uncomfortable.

Another reason that could lead the XA's to see the YB's as soft was related to the fact that the YB adherents tended to feel overresponsible for causing others to behave incompetently. If A were authoritarian, the YB adherents might spend an inordinate amount of time asking what they were doing that may have made A behave authoritarianly.

"I think that my feelings of responsibility for the development of others are limitless," said one. "Yes," said another, "but they must end somewhere." "Yes," said the first, "you are correct. I guess I work hard to make certain that if the other individual fails, he has done so because of his own lack of competence and not because I am doing something that makes him less effective."

The interventionist asked if the clients had discussed these feelings with the XA adherents. Perhaps the XA adherents behaved in a controlling manner because they, too, felt overresponsible. The YB's reacted to overresponsibility by looking within and the XA's by looking outward. Perhaps one way to deal with overresponsibility is to talk openly about the lack of confidence that existed among the clients.

"I'd like to do that," said one of the YB adherents, "but you know I can hear———saying, 'What the hell are we talking about this for? It's just a lot of bunk.'" He was immediately supported by the other two.

The interventionist then asked if it were not correct to conclude that they were being controlled by the fears and dissatisfactions of others. Also their position implied an *underdeveloped* feeling of responsibility about themselves. Why do they feel hesitant about insisting that, for them, a discussion about overresponsibility is not bunk?

The executives agreed that this explanation was plausible. It underscored for them the validity of their conclusion that they were not going to continue to live with these differences. They also agreed that they were not asking the XA adherents for unilateral conformity. They wanted an opportunity to discuss and work through these issues. What they were not going to accept any longer was the notion that their feelings and ideas were bunk and irrelevant to the effective operation of the organization.

Nor were they going to go into the confrontation with the expectation that change should occur quickly or that a complete managerial philosophy and design would emerge. Both would be unrealistic. However, they were becoming increasingly clear of certain minimal conditions about which they felt strongly. As one man said, "I can live with life being less than complete and imperfect. Lord knows I represent both. But I cannot live with closedness, manipulation, and intellectual dishonesty, my own or others'."

The more the executives discussed these issues, the more aware they became of the number of times during actual business meetings when they had suppressed their urge to question certain managerial practices that were being recommended because they did not want to create a situation that coerced the XA adherents to examine their interpersonal relationships, which would be seen by the XA's as unfair and could lead to further defensiveness within the system.

Another insight that surfaced was that in addition to withholding comments relevant to XA adherents, they withheld comments about their own behavior, especially when they were behaving inconsistently. They did so because they felt the group norms against such discussions. However, they would tend to meet as a subgroup and discuss these issues. This strategy tended to have two unintended consequences. If they behaved inconsistently with their philosophy, the probability was quite high that the XA adherents noticed the inconsistency. Since none of the YB adherents discussed the inconsistency openly, the XA adherents could infer that the YB adherents did not genuinely believe in their views and did not really confront each other, then why should they confront them?

The second unintended consequence was that XA adherents could use this lack of confrontation as another indication that YB meant a soft management philosophy. This attitude returns us to the point with which this section began, and we have closed the cycle.

6. Vacillation and uncertainty

In addition to the finding from these experiences that the transition period is a long one, there is the finding of an extended period of vacillation and uncertainty, of progress and regression.

Given the analysis above, the length and turbulence of the transition period is understandable. Not only were major changes being requested in interpersonal and group behavior, leadership style, and organizational design, there were also fundamental questions regarding the alteration of the subordinates' attitudes. In systems B and C, the top management were unanimous in their perceptions that the previous managements had created some very deep-seated attitudes on the part of the subordinates, at all levels, of dependence, withdrawal or apathy, aggression, and hostility. The nonrecognition of self-responsibility and personal causation was even stronger at lower levels. It would take many years to unfreeze these attitudes, still more to develop new ones, and still more to find processes by which to reinforce them.

If the experiences of client systems A and B are generalizable, it can be said with a good degree of safety that change will not come through the constant input of information or the mechanics of persuasion. Change will come slowly as a result of the members in problem-solving or decision-making conferences being permitted to confront the new values, their superiors, their peers, and their subordinates; constantly monitoring and correcting every move; periodically reacting with frustrations, anger, and withdrawal at the difficulties involved.

In client system C, for example, vacillation and testing began with the president who was one of the most dedicated adherents to change and development. He was not always clear as to how he should react; how to design new managerial methods, new structures, new rewards and penalty systems; how to respond to elation as well as to depression, his own or others. Nor were the OD specialists able to make suggestions that satisfied even their own aspirations. Again and again we come smack up against the barrier of lack of tested knowledge.

The lower one went down the organization, the more magnified became the attitudes toward organizational development. Those who feared it feared it strongly and usually withdrew or did not cooperate to make it more effective. Those who believed in its value were enthusiastic supporters to the point, in some cases, of becoming true believers. Many expressed impatience with the top for not moving faster. It was the writer's impression that some of the younger, lower-level, and more impatient executives would have reduced their impatience if they were placed in the position of being responsible to the board of directors and stockholders. The top, on the other hand, wanted to move faster. However, they were tied up in Gordian knots of their interpersonal and group dynamics, heavily weighted down by their deep sense of loyalty and responsibility which, as we have shown, caused them to move cautiously.

There was another factor that may be worth serious consideration. The insistence of the top management in organization C to move carefully and to accept only tested policies helped to prevent theory Y from becoming an ideology to which people would be required to adhere. An ideology could become coercive and would tend to be impervious to data regarding its ineffectiveness. The more closed it was to feedback, the lower the probability that it could become self-corrective and adaptive to future changing conditions.

Because of the difficulties described above and because of the vacillation and ambivalence, individuals and groups became more difficult to predict. There developed the issue of trust. Could individuals be trusted to behave consistently with the new values, especially under conditions of overload, pressure, and ambiguity? The answer, for each individual, tended to be one of uncertainty. Partially, the uncertainty came from the very unpredictableness of people's reactions and behavior. But another important cause was their own awareness that they could not trust themselves to behave consistently. This lack of self-trust became particularly perplexing to those who were working hardest to make the program successful. Why should they show such inconsistency when they were so genuinely convinced of the new theory? Unfortunately, neither their learning at the laboratories nor the OD professionals helped them to develop a realistic level of aspiration or an understanding that such mistrust is to be expected because it is caused by genuine uncertainty and ambiguity of the best roads toward success.

One reason the OD professionals were not as helpful was that they too were impatient for change and anxious for signs of progress. They had come to the conclusion that without progress the program — and their jobs — might be in jeopardy.

7. The resiliency of pattern B behavior

One of the unexpected findings of the study is related to the resilience of pattern B behavior. The YB subgroup in organization B felt continually attacked and rarely had opportunities to practice their newly learned behavior. Yet, when they met as a subgroup, with and without the interventionist, they would strive to behave as much as they could congruently with YB. In the case of organization C, many of the executives had learned in their laboratory experiences to behave somewhat competently in a manner approximating YB. However, because of reasons described previously, they were unable to create the conditions in their group to utilize their newly achieved competence. Thus the new behavior received little reinforcement. Yet, when the interventionist entered their group, they were able to alter their behavior significantly toward YB and return to XA as soon as he left.

Pattern B, according to these executives, is intrinsically satisfying. Even though the overwhelming forces in the present may act to extinguish it, they do not succeed. At best the pattern is suppressed until individuals can create conditions under which the pattern can be surfaced.

8. Questions to consider seriously about going from XA to YB

During the course of interviews and observations with the executives, several of them raised questions that they would advise others to discuss thoroughly with their group before they embarked on a program for organizational development. Most of the questions were related to the problem of commitment to the program and the fears and tensions that it would arouse if genuine change was to occur.

(a) Is top management aware that they are about to undertake an experiment? Do they realize that very little is known about effective organizational development and that every step they take will be full of risk? Are they aware that there are no major full-fledged success stories of organizational development in any kind of organization?

(b) Is top management aware of the costs of failure? Are they aware that once begun, organizational development is difficult to stop? Individuals' aspirations are raised and their hopes are kindled when they believe that the quality of their life within the organization may be bettered. To call a halt to such a program would be to run the risk of confirming to everyone—especially the young and those of any age who are most involved—that the organization is unable or unwilling to find ways of making organizational life more meaningful.

Can organizations of the future afford not to change their basic ideas and practices of how to manage human resources? Does not the ultimate cost of failure go beyond the individual case to the existing philosophy of management and system of enterprise?

(c) Is the commitment deep enough to deflect feelings of guilt when failure has occurred and to strengthen conviction to experiment anew when the "sure answer" becomes, at best, a sure question or a wrong lead and, at worst, an added contribution to frustration, tension, and divisiveness?

(d) Is the top management united enough to overcome the period of counterproductiveness and to resist reverting to the old style of leadership? If it is predictable that regressions will occur, it is equally predictable that if the regression becomes policy it will disillusion those internally committed to change and strengthen those who fear it.

(e) Is the top management committed enough so that it will be able to live with and effectively overcome internal conflict and intergroup warfare that could lead to a house divided? Will it strive to perceive the many shades of gray instead of the blacks and whites it will be pressed to consider? And is it ready to value ambiguity and dilemma as a source for organizational development rather than as experiences to be blotted out, lest people become too upset?

(f) How does top management cope with the fact that they are experimenting with basic changes in societal values and behavior ingrained in individuals as, if not more, deeply than any other known to man? Are they ready to cope with executives who will expect quick results? What will they say to the disbelievers who demand tangible intellectual proof of the validity and practicality of the changes when none exists and, even if it did, would not resolve their anxiety?

(g) Is the management ready to face the aloneness and fear that come with any experiment that focuses on changing some of the most basic values in the society? Moreover, are they aware that the difficulties are compounded by the fact that management will probably not be permitted to experiment by giving up responsibility for

the continued safe and effective operation of their system in a world that either disavows YB or is unaware of it, or, in a few cases, overloves it to the point that it becomes an ideology rather than a theory of management? Is the top management ready to live with the continual pushing and pulling, as John Gardner has put it, "the uncritical lover and the unloving critic?"

Theory Y and pattern B may be, as we pointed out in the previous chapter, resilient and intrinsically satisfying, yet it should be clear that they do not come at a cheap price. The high price indicates the genuine involvement that is required. The high price is also a safeguard that society has against the unauthentic use of theory Y and the skin-surface acceptance of pattern B.

Chapter six
Conclusions II:
Organizational Development
and Effective Intervention

1. Some guideposts about effective intervention activities during the transition period

(a) The primary tasks of valid information, free choice, and internal commitment became especially important during the transition. Given. the vacillation, ambiguity, pain, frustration that go with the transition, it was important and difficult for the client system to develop valid information, free choice, and internal commitment. Yet, these very tasks in the eyes of the skeptics at all levels became the criteria for judging progress and the genuineness of the motives of the people "up top" to the new values of management.

(b) The very vacillation and uncertainty that became a

problem also became the source for change. These conditions provided a rich resource of inconsistent and incongruent behavior or behavior and values that were inconsistent. Such inconsistencies, when surfaced, tended to create a sense of tension in individuals who had a need to be competent and a sense of constructive intent toward their fellow man. This tension became the motivation for individuals to seek more information, to strive harder to design free choices, and to develop internal commitment to their choices.

(c) In a turbulent world of transition, it is important for the interventionist to have thought through the implications of many of the questions that clients tend to ask. For example, if confronted with the issue of theory Y being soft management he can use previous research to give him clues as to where theory X is soft to help the individuals examine the fears behind the accusation of soft management or the possible projections involved. If confronted with a request for an assurance that no one can get hurt in a T-group, he should be prepared to give his evaluation of the group *and* point out that the only guarantee that is meaningful is based upon the concern and trust they have for each other. If asked to help design new organizational structures, administrative controls, or reward and penalty systems, the interventionist can bring to bear ideas and issues derived from the theorizing and (admittedly, all too meager) empirical research.

In these examples, the interventionist is cast in the role of being a spokesman for the theory, research, and practice related to the problems of transition. He is asked to be authoritative, without being authoritarian; to be confronting, without being punitive; to be clear, without becoming didactic. In short, it may be legitimate for the interventionist to be authoritative and to create the conditions where others can question and confront his views and behavior.

(d) In being authoritative, however, the interventionist is not being asked to make decisions for the clients about choices that are their responsibility. The interventionist also has to be especially careful about the dependency issue. During the period of turbulent transition it is understandable that clients will attempt to become dependent upon him for suggestions and solutions to their problems. As in case C, the interventionist confronted the clients with their attempts to make him responsible for decisions that were theirs to make. This led the clients to accept further their own responsibility.

(e) One of the major tasks of the interventionist in all client systems was to help the clients become aware of their role in causing the problems which they were attempting to overcome. Accurate awareness of personal causation is a necessary but not sufficient factor in effective individual or organizational development. Unless the executives' role in causing problems is clearly understood, it is easy to develop solutions that bypass their incompetences.

Let us illustrate these points with excerpts from a meeting observed by the interventionist. The session began with the chairman reviewing the agenda. The group had committed itself to bring ideas of how to increase interdepartmental effectiveness and to make more clear the accountability and responsibility of each department. He then said, "The floor is open." A period of silence ensued. H said to B, "You were the one to suggest this idea originally, you begin." B was visibly surprised and commented, "Lucky me."

The interventionist intervened and asked if it were a group norm or practice for someone to select the individual who makes a suggestion to begin discussing it. He may not be the best man to begin and, moreover, he does not feel responsible for his participation. In the long run, such practice may also inhibit others from making suggestions unless they are ready to be coerced into implementing them effectively. This norm could reduce the production of new ideas, or it could be used by manipulators as a way to gain control over the discussion.

Even though all these possibilities are relevant, it is important for the interventionist first to produce valid information about the group's practice and about the members' feelings toward silence, because discomfort with silence would easily produce the need to coerce others into talking.

Two executives responded that they were not uncomfortable with silence, yet silence wasn't productive. Two more added that silence did make them uncomfortable. Another three questioned whether the most productive way to end a silence was to select someone who may not be ready to speak. Still another individual pointed out that this norm may increase the silence period because people may be waiting to be selected.

> INT.: I should like to recommend that you develop a norm or practice that encourages the individual to be responsible for his own decision to participate.
> A: I think that would be more helpful.
> C: Funny, I never noticed that this was our practice.
> E: Oh, yeah, I've noticed it. You put the bee on somebody else to absolve you.
> F: At the last meeting G asked J to define————. This was a nice way of passing the buck.
> INT.: Recall that incident for a moment. Did others feel that was a way about G?
> *(Six men nodded their heads affirmatively or said "yes.")*
> INT.: This could have been important information.

G: It would have been for me; I did it because I thought I was helping J.

The discussion led to an analysis of the process by which they made decisions. The group concluded that they had not studied the process before and that they had systematic ways of discussing decisions. This led to an exploration of the members' responsibility in the group for its effectiveness. The conclusion was that again this had not been worked through.

Someone then pointed out that the same problem existed in the organization. Many people assumed that the responsibility for actions was not clear. The result was that people took or gave away the responsibility, depending upon which strategy would help them survive best.

About a half-hour later an episode was discussed that represented a crucial breakdown in cooperation between two key departments. The head of one (Mr. F) said, "The reason we got fouled up was that we tried to work it out together. We tried our OD approach and it didn't work." *(laughter)*

The interventionist asked, "What is it that happened that was in line with OD that prevented progress?"

F: Well, I don't think he intended to prevent progress. . . . *(continued)*

INT.: I am asking a different question. As I understood it, you felt that G would not go along with what you thought was the correct action; furthermore that your preferred way of handling it was to say, "Look here, I am the expert in this, do it as I say; and finally, you decided against doing so because of the spirit of participation and OD, correct?

F: Yes.

INT.: I am trying to understand the meaning that participation and OD have for you and others. For me, it would mean that I would talk to G about my perception of his resistance and work that through. I would characterize your behavior as "diplomatic" and not open.

The discussions continued with G admitting that he realized F saw him as a resister. He would not talk about this openly because F was not open. (Note that each was holding the other responsible for his closedness.) Both F and G decided (privately) that the other was not influenceable and that the matter would have to go to the president. This is an example of an unresolved intergroup problem being passed to the top.

The interventionist pointed out, "This is not my view of OD. That is using the concept in a way that is foreign to me." There followed a discussion that perhaps they were using OD as a scapegoat. A pointed out, and C, D, E, and G agreed that, in effect, F and G were being "soft" because they were not confronting the relevant issues.

The interventionist then noted:

(a) Effective organizational development was being misperceived.

(b) F and G (and others) were not being open and confronting issues constructively. In this sense they were being "soft."

(c) Since this "soft" behavior was attributed to the motivation of following OD, then OD was seen as being "soft management."

(d) The interventionist's strategy of being open might have prevented the three month delays or the buckpassing to the top.

This discussion prompted A to return to the first problem discussed (turnover) and admit that he did not agree with C's analysis. "I just think that C had made an inference without any specifics to back him up."

INT.: Are you concerned about how he made that inference?

A: No, that would be up to him.

INT.: Why? Another scenario might be to tell C, "I don't understand how you arrived at the view that it is turnover." This could give you the raw data upon which his analysis is based.

A: I guess I was more annoyed at him than anything else.

At the end of this discussion on group process A asked if the group was ready to return to the substantive issues. Two executives said "yes," the rest remained silent. A then said, "OK, I'll go back to the substance, and if you have questions you ask them."

INT.: I should like to ask why aren't more individuals stating openly how they feel?

G: What if you are not sure?

INT.: That would be important information.

B: Isn't silence passive agreement?

INT.: It could be; it also could be the opposite. Silence is difficult to code accurately. Also, if silence is used as a way to proceed, the manipulator could take advantage and take over, while the person who withdraws from responsibility could easily withdraw since, in this case, A took over.

Another bit of evidence comes from a crude content analysis of the typescript of the discussion. The interventionist noted that most of the behavior was not facilitative. For example:

The nature of the episodes	The number of episodes
1. Requiring individuals who raise a question to answer it..............	5
2. Developing no overtly accepted mode of discussing and problem solving a particular decision.....................	4
3. Individuals who did not level with	

each other about important substantive
issues.   7
    4. Individuals who privately held differ-
ent views about group process and the mo-
tives of others in saying what they did. . . .   9

One striking result of even such a simple, crude analysis
is the amount of behavior that occurred that was dysfunctional to problem solving of substantive issues and to
effective decision making. All these men had some laboratory experience. In fairness, it should be pointed out that
one reason the interventionist was able to surface the lack
of openness, the differences of perception, the inconsistencies in group effectiveness was that the men *had* learned
to identify these phenomena and were able and willing to
do so when asked. This would not be as easy with an un-
trained group.

However, one may also raise the question if they have
been trained enough. The points surfaced by the analysis
are elementary and basic. Giving and receiving valid information in ways that encourage further openness and
experimentation and developing effective group decision-
making processes are basic issues. The fact that they are
so basic does not mean that they are easy to learn. Indeed,
here we have a group that has the support of professional
OD experts, and yet they have not mastered these skills.

Speaking of the OD professional, the top executives commented after this meeting that they wished their professionals would be more confronting with them when they
sit in on their meetings. They found the OD people to be
"too soft" on the executives. Again we find this issue of
softness arising. Interviews with six of these members
suggested that they were somewhat disappointed with
their OD group because they did not point out group processes adequately. They seemed to range from aggressive
(sometimes hostile) needlers to unsure, somewhat apolo-

getic interveners. Both extremes were seen as indicating
that the OD professionals were, at times, defensive and/or
uncomfortable about their role. In the writer's view the
executives were only partially correct. The OD specialists
had many organizational blocks to overcome that had been
created by the executives.

Did the executives communicate their feelings to the
OD professionals? Apparently not. How could the OD people be expected to change if this information was not being
given to them? Moreover, such a confrontation might have
produced new information from the OD people. For example, they may not have perceived their behavior as did some
of the executives. Here is an example of top management
being "soft" (i.e., not being open with their OD people)
and yet accusing the OD people of being soft (i.e., not
being open with them).

The executives in this case were willing to be confronted.
This did not mean that they would agree with every intervention, nor did they expect that the OD men had to be
correct all the time. The most important requirement they
would make of the OD men seemed to be that they be consistent, relatively unconflicted about their values, and
behave effectively, especially when they are challenging
the behavioral competence of others.

2. Requirements for effective
change strategy

Implicit in the analysis to date is the assumption that effective change occurs when the changes are long lasting,
when they are self-monitoring, and when they are reinforcing of system competence and lead to further system
development. These criteria are, as we have seen, very difficult to achieve. The difficulty stems from the conditions

created by the pattern A world and the, at times, antagonistic conditions required if pattern B is to emerge. Pattern A, in short, does not tend to create the potential nor the competence in its members to seek to explore pattern B conditions. Stating the position in the form of an hypothesis it would be that the more committed the client system members are to pattern A, the less they will value the conditions implicit in pattern B and the more difficult it will be for them to move toward pattern B.

Let us specify the thinking behind this hypothesis in more detail. In Figure 2 we note five dimensions. They represent five dimensions along which one can identify the effectiveness of change. Any change that is consistent with the basic pyramidal structure and/or pattern A will tend to be low on all these dimensions. Any changes that attempt to design new and more organic structures, as well as pattern B-type relationships, will fall on the high end of these dimensions.

For example, a change at the interpersonal, group, intergroup, or organizational levels that approximates the values in pattern B and theory Y will tend to be highly deviant from the existing cultural and system norms. The

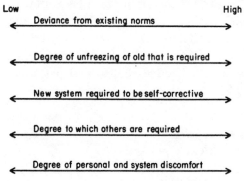

Figure 2. Conditions for Effective Change

degree of unfreezing necessary will be much greater than if the change remained within the basic assumptions of theory Y and values of pattern B. In pattern A changes, the system typically has the changes imposed upon it. Thus the commitment to *self-corrective* (as differentiated from others such as management or staff groups) behavior is low; in YB it would be high. Moreover YB changes require the feedback of others. One cannot mastermind his own changes and play his cards close to his chest. Finally, the personal and systemic discomfort will tend to be highest for YB changes and lowest for XA changes, since the former tend to be antagonistic to the latter, thereby creating a threat for the client system and its members.

This analysis suggests a reinterpretation may be necessary of the criteria for effective change recently suggested by several behavioral scientists. For example, *(a)* organizations B and C were under pressure to improve; *(b)* the management experienced difficulty in coping with the pressures; *(c)* the top management were emotionally committed to effective change; *(d)* the top management spent much time in clarifying working relationships; *(e)* the top executives assumed direct and highly involved roles in implementing the changes; and *(f)* the top focused on continual experimentation with change. These are all criteria supposedly associated with effective change (Greiner, 1965). In short, B and C meet almost all of Greiner's criteria for effective change, and yet effective change had not been occurring.

3. Should changes begin with structural factors or with interpersonal factors?[6]

One of the continuing dialogues in the field is related to the relative effectiveness of the different strategies for an effective system. Some suggest that change may be more effective if one begins with structural changes, while others suggest the interpersonal relationships (or groups or intergroup) should be the point of initial attack.

Our view is that each position is valid under a given set of conditions. We would hypothesize that the more the change being considered is at the low end of the six dimensions, the higher the probability the structural changes will be effective without previous changes in interpersonal behavior and values (because personal causation and responsibility are low). If one examines the literature on structural changes that have been reported to be effective without initial changes in interpersonal relationships, one notes that they were instituted at the *lower* levels of the hierarchy and that they may be identified as being at the low end of the dimensions in our model.

For example, Trist and others (1962) developed changes in the coal mines, not by altering the new technology, but by altering the composition to fit the new technology. Blau and Scott (1962) recommended that a procedural manual be used by the case workers to reduce the advice sought by case workers from each other. The basic technology again was not altered.

An apparent contradiction with our view exists with the work of Ford (1969). He indicates that job enlargement in certain white collar jobs may increase morale and productivity and decrease absenteeism. Note, first, that the success was with employees who were at the lower levels of the organization and who had little interdependence

---

[6] As this book went to press, I became aware of a manuscript (also in press) that discusses these issues in more detail: Harvey A. Hornstein, Barbara A. Benedict, Warner Burke, Marion Hornstein, and Roy J. Lewicki, *Strategies of Social Intervention*, The Free Press, New York, 1971.

with other workers. They were largely individual contributors. Also, in terms of our theory, Ford was able to redesign the job to increase the personal causation (responsibility) the girls experienced at work. This is precisely what one wishes to be able to do at the upper level. The objective of the top management in organizations B and C was to increase the experience of personal causation by going toward YB. However, the critical factors that prevented effective change were interpersonal, group, and intergroup factors.

Some suggest that sophisticated management-information systems may be a way to coerce new behavior on the part of top management. In the writer's experience MIS are greatly resisted by management who believe that the degree of personal responsibility and challenge that is implicit in their job (and they have to fight continuously to protect in pattern A world) may be significantly reduced (Argyris, 1971). Moreover, where these systems may be designed to increase personal responsibility, challenge, and experimentation the existing (pattern A) interpersonal relationships seem to mask and eventually suppress these potentialities (Argyris, 1967).

Recently Wohlking (1969) cited the experimental work on communication networks, on attitude change, and on enforced behavior change by requiring whites and blacks to work together. Given the recent research on the demand characteristics of experimental situations, one should be careful in suggesting that their results are applicable to nonexperimental settings. Moreover, there are other cautions to be considered. Different structures do induce different behavior and morale; but the experimental research has not focused on how to gain internal commitment to changes in structures. The subjects who had their attitudes altered by inducing them to make public statements (in role-playing situations) changed attitudes that had nothing to do with their jobs, their pay, their survival in the system, or the taking on of a significantly greater sense of commitment toward work. Finally Pettigrew's notion that attitudes toward blacks can be changed by requiring whites to interact with blacks may be the case because, as he points out, the change is in the direction of legally accepted and (increasingly so) societally sanctioned norms (Pettigrew, 1958).

To summarize, the critical factor that one has to examine is the one of personal causation and responsibility. If that is low, then externally induced change (e.g., changes in organizational structure) will tend to be effective. Presently, such changes would especially be effective at the lower levels of organization and where the job requirements control human behavior. Where effective change does depend upon individuals' personal responsibility, changes in interpersonal relationships, group effectiveness, and intergroup relationships are necessary before structural changes can be introduced.

The writer would add another reason why the more effective sequence in making change is first to focus on personal causation and then on causation by other factors. There is, to put it simply, very little empirically supported knowledge about how to change organizational structures or administrative controls.[7] Consequently, the changes will probably be primitive and will require continual monitoring by the individuals. Continual monitoring requires

---

[7] For some suggestions see R. Likert, *The Human Organization,* McGraw-Hill Book Company, New York, 1967; Alfred J. Marrow, David G. Bowers, Stanley E. Seashore, *Management by Participation,* Harper & Row, Publishers, Incorporated, New York, 1967; and the author's *Integrating the Individual and the Organization,* John Wiley & Sons, Inc., New York, 1964.

internal commitment, and internal commitment develops when individuals are internally motivated to design and execute their own changes. But, can defensive individuals design minimally defensive-producing external stimuli? The writer has concluded, to date, that it is doubtful.

The position is based upon three working assumptions. First, given the criteria of system competence, effective change means that the problems are solved in such a way that they remain solved, and this is accomplished without reducing the present level of effectiveness of the system (it is hoped, enhancing it). Second, no matter at what level of analysis a change is begun, it will influence all the other levels. For example, a change begun at the interpersonal level will eventually lead to changes at the group and/or structural levels and vice versa. Third, change is most effective when it deals with the factors that have the greatest causal influence on the problem in question. In some problem areas organizational structure may play a greater causal role than group processes; in others the opposite is true.

Drawing from present organizational research, the following generalization may be used as a guidepost in searching for the most important factors. The further one goes down the hierarchy, the higher the probability that the potent variables will be found in the technology, administrative controls, and organizational structure. The higher one goes up the hierarchy, the greater the probability that the potent variables will be found in interpersonal and group relations (perhaps administrative controls if one thinks of financial controls).

To put this another way, the more personal causation is involved in the changes, the greater the probability that interpersonal relationships will be involved. However, this need not be the case. To ask European executives to remove their children from the board involves little be-havioral change on the part of the executive. However, this structural change has many personal roots which would have to be explored and worked through if the executive will freely choose and be internally committed to eliminating his children from the board.

This illustration reminds us of the argument that some-times the most potent factors may be the most difficult to change. Some suggest that under these conditions, it may be necessary to begin a change activity with the less potent factors which are less threatening to the client system. Elsewhere the writer has discussed the dangers in this strategy. Some are *(a)* the subordinates tend to feel that the change activities are not getting at the key factors, and *(b)* the interventionists have been unduly influenced by the same anxieties that operate to inhibit the clients from dealing with the potent factors, which leads to *(c)* a sense of pessimism about the probabilities for successful change, which, in turn, *(d)* may reduce the commitment necessary for successful change (thereby producing a self-fulfilling failure). The interventionist who is aware of these dangers and decides to take the roundabout approach precisely for these reasons may find later on that he has placed himself in a bind. There may come a time when he believes the most important thing for the clients to do is to face up to their problems openly. At the moment, the clients may retort that when the interventionist had dif-ficulties, when he was under stress, he decided to take a less open and more devious approach. All they are now doing is emulating his behavior and not his words. [This suggests that if a less open and direct route has to be taken, it may be wise to be frank about the reasons for the strat-egy (Argyris, 1970).]

There is another important issue that requires closer

examination. It involves the question of the definition of the problem. Let us examine several changes that are frequently made and accepted by individuals as a result of OD programs.

A will check with B before he makes certain decisions that involve B's group.

A will meet with B, at least once a year, to evaluate B's performance.

If A follows through on both of these recommendations, his behavior will have changed in that he will be talking and informing B (in case A) and exploring evaluations (in case B).

Many interventionists are satisfied if they can help to introduce such changes in the system. They believe "the problems" are now solved. From our point of view, only one set of problems may have been resolved. A may check with B before he makes decisions, but the behavior involved in checking may permit B no more influence than he had before A ever checked with B. Under these conditions B may be worse off. In the second case, A may meet with B for a performance review, but the dynamics during that meeting may lead to increasing relationship difficulties [apparently, a not too uncommon experience in many management-performance review sessions (Meyer, Kay, and French, 1965)].

In both of these cases the problems, therefore, were not solved in such a way that they remained solved or that the present level of problem-solving effectiveness was maintained. For these criteria to be fulfilled, A and B will have to learn new behaviors that are closer to YB than XA. Such changes are not easy to make. They require changes that tend toward the right ends of the continua described above.

Such behavioral changes require at least three levels of

input. They require *(a)* emotional insights into the self
(especially one's defense and coping mechanisms), *(b)*
cognitive maps of the new and presumably more effective
behavior plus the paths to learning such behavior, and
(c) practice in unfreezing the old defensive and coping
mechanisms and the incorporating of the new behavior.

If one may judge from the executives' (in cases B and
C) description of their laboratory experiences, they were
primarily designed to achieve the first input, namely emotional insights into self and others. There was a little cognitive input on new and more effective behavior. There was
almost no concentrated effort on practicing in developing
the new skills. Thus, those who learned from their experiences reported that, at best, they became more aware of
their own and others' interpersonal difficulties; they developed a deeper appreciation for the requirements of a
change, a desire to design new and more competent systems. However, they also reported that they left the laboratory lacking the maps or the skills necessary for these new
changes to be designed and instituted. One may raise questions about the advisability of designing laboratories that
produce such uneven or incomplete changes. But this question may not be fair. To produce awareness of self and
others is very difficult indeed. How much can one expect
a one-week laboratory to accomplish?

4. Dilemmas of the OD professional's role

In this connection it may be instructive to examine the
experiences in organization C, which had the most ad-
vanced OD program and staff. The examination will focus
on some important laboratory programs that they designed

for some key executive managers. In planning these pro-grams the OD specialists were concerned about the de-pendence issue. They wanted the executives to become masters of their own growth as quickly as possible. They were willing to join the TMG to do some group processing. However, they also urged the TMG to move as quickly as possible to the point where they did their own group pro-cessing. In this connection, they recommended the taping of the TMG sessions and selective listening to the tapes. The executives agreed to the tape recording. However, few listened to the tapes systematically.

Is this the appropriate strategy toward the TMG? Why does it make sense to assume that they can analyze their own behavior effectively, since they are unable to behave effectively with each other? How can a group composed of competitive executives who tended not to listen to each other; who tended to be highly evaluative and attributive; who felt their group was highly ineffective and who felt somewhat helpless to alter it; who were ambivalent about their own competence, etc., be able to make effective changes by themselves?

Asking these questions may raise the question, "Why would the OD specialists define their role in the manner just described?" The writer does not have complete data on this point. It could be that the OD group was more uncom-fortable and somewhat more threatened (organizationally) by working with the top. This may have been the case with some OD members, but it is doubtful that it was the case for all.

Three more likely causes may be *(a)* their concept of an executive-change strategy which makes top-management dependence on OD specialists an undesirable phenome-non, *(b)* their own difficulty to model directly observable behavior that was minimally evaluative and attributive, and *(c)* their lack of cognitive maps about how an organization may alter organizational factors in order to move from XA to YB.

It is being suggested, therefore, that the strategy developed by the inside OD group may be partially based upon an awareness of their limitations, an awareness that tended to be more implicit than explicit. The fear that one will not be as effective as one wishes is a fear that exists for most professionals, including the writer. We genuinely want to be helpful and to make real progress, yet we are painfully aware of (1) the lack of education and training available and (2) the enormous complexity of organizational development activities, especially the barriers that have to be overcome.

The complexity involved in being an effective OD professional is not to be minimized. His is one of the most difficult roles in our society. Helping anxious executives to change basic values, ingrained behavior, and important aspects of culture that support these values is not easy, especially if there is the fear (identified by line executives themselves in the previous chapter) that management can give up prematurely and cause unfortunate regression and painful tensions within the system.

A recent analysis of the role of an OD professional makes explicit how difficult his job may be (Argyris, 1970). For example, the interventionist is in a world full of:

1. Three major discrepancies:

(a) Discrepancy between his own and the client's views on causes of problems and designs for effective organizations

(b) Discrepancy between his own and the client's views on effective implementation of change

(c) Discrepancy between his own ideals and what he is able to deliver in reality

2. This gives the interventionist membership in two overlapping but different worlds where he has to face:

(a) Continual mistrust

(b) Minimal feedback about his own effectiveness

3. These conditions require that the interventionist:

(a) Have a high degree of confidence in his philosophy of intervention

(b) Perceive accurately stressful reality

(c) Accept client's attacks and mistrust

(d) Trust in his own experience in spite of loneliness and realization of the likely deviancy of his position

(e) Be able to behave, as much as possible, in a minimally evaluative, minimally attributive, minimally inconsistent manner, even though the clients may behave primarily in an evaluative, attributive, and inconsistent manner and tend to charge those who do not do the same as being "soft."

As to the educational experiences available to individuals who wish to become professional interventionists, several universities and the NTL Institute for Applied Behavioral Sciences have designed several courses ranging from one week to six months. They are helpful, but inadequate, given the task of the interventionist.

I believe that the role of the interventionist in our society is about where the role of the medical doctor was in the early 1700s. However, as research produces more knowledge, and as the potential of an effective professional interventionist is understood, full-fledged degree-granting programs will be created that will match the opportunities available, the rigor required, and the long-range dedication necessary if one wishes to become a medical doctor.

If I would fault the existing programs, it is because none of them focus adequately on developing effective interpersonal competence of the kind described above. Moreover, too little is being done in developing appropriate new organizational designs.

As we have noted before and will repeat several times, these two levels of competence and knowledge are extremely important. The executive who has just returned from a successful laboratory experience has, at best, developed a genuine desire to develop new personal skills and to consider new organizational designs. He requires OD specialists who can help him in these areas. In the case of the interpersonal competence he needs to interact with OD specialists who confront him when he is not behaving competently and who themselves are able to model competent behavior (e.g., minimally evaluative and attributive). In the case of organizational designs, he requires help from specialists who are familiar with the issues involved, the dangers inherent in, and the range of choices the literature suggests are available to bring about more effective systems. We are *not* suggesting that top management expects clear-cut definitive answers in issues of organizational change. Today's sophisticated executives are well aware of the complexity involved in changing organizations and the primitive state of the literature. They would probably mistrust an interventionist who appeared to have a panacea. The thoughtful and sophisticated executives who have decided to involve their system in a long-range OD program (as in B and C) tend to prefer OD specialists who understand organizations so well that they can help the top management develop realistic experimental plans rather than final designs.

In the writer's experience both of these competences require much time and effort to develop. It is no exaggeration to suggest that an interventionist can legitimately spend the *majority* of his time developing his interpersonal skills and new maps about organizational effectiveness and change. The more competent they are in these areas, the more progress they may help to bring about in the remaining time when they are working with the client system.

I should like to try to develop more credence for this view by turning to the second activity which the OD people in organization C had executed. This was a laboratory program where key executive groups met to focus on learning about interpersonal and group issues while beginning to identify key substantial organizational issues. The groups were composed of executives who had important organizational relationships with each other, but in no case was their immediate superior in attendance. Also, whenever possible the group was seeded with at least one executive who had been to a laboratory. The hope was that he would help to facilitate group process and problem solving.

Why this design? Because the OD people wanted to maximize the degree to which the members would learn from each other, to minimize trainer dependence, to maximize the use of the small number of trainers available (relative to the group being trained). On the basis of some pilot experiences and interviews the OD group believed that this model would be effective and would generate internal commitment to more OD work.

The two most important results were that the majority of the executives found the program interesting and helpful. However, the expected request for more help on OD issues did not materialize. Why?

Unfortunately no data were collected that could provide a systematic basis to answer this question. Thus we are limited to anecdotal data and speculation.

The writer met with the majority of the OD groups to discuss their OD programs. He learned that they had two basic foundations to their change strategy: minimal intervention in the quasi-T-groups (the OD people visited the groups systematically "to take their temperature"); and the more emotional involvement by the executives, the better.

If the analysis made up to this point is valid, then we may again ask the question, "Why did the OD people assume that individuals can eventually learn to discuss substantive organizational issues without having been able to develop the behavioral competence implicit in YB?" Moreover, given the difficulty TMG members had in behaving effectively with each other (after they had been through successful experiential programs) why was it assumed that the next lower-level executives could become as or more effective, especially with a significantly shorter period of learning and without the help of interventionists?

The answers to these questions can only be conjectures. But, again it is suggested that the design for this laboratory experience may have been based on the anxieties identified above (lack of own high personal competence and maps about effective organizational changes).

There are some interesting indirect data available on this point. The writer asked members of the OD group to describe, if the millennium were reached, how they hoped their clients would behave. Their response was that their clients would be able to behave more openly, to generate more trust, etc. The writer then asked for some illustrations of such behavior. The interesting aspect about all the illustrations was that they were attributive and evaluative. Thus the OD professionals' conception of what they wished for their clients would still be behavior that was part of pattern A. For example:

(a) "I would like for an individual to stop saying to

people such things as, 'You're a loudmouth,' and be able to say something like, 'You're talking so much that you don't want to hear my idea.'"

(b) "In my early years as an OD man I would communicate hostility in my T-group. I turned people off because of my tone, which would convey that I was rejecting them. Now I am able to say to someone (in a much less threatening way) something like, 'You're just not listening to what we're saying!'"

Another bit of evidence that suggests our analysis may have some validity is that the expected request for more OD experiences did not materialize, nor, as one of the OD men stated it, "were we able to do something which would continue to raise the openness and confidence in the back-home situation."

Why is this so? If our hypothesis that people are not going to change their pattern A behavior significantly under these conditions is correct, then the new found openness was probably related more to the support generated by going to a laboratory experience and the appropriate interventions of the OD people than to skills the participants learned. If so, then why would one expect increased openness and confidence in the back-home situation? After all, the back-home situation is not conceptualized as a learning situation nor one where the OD people are expected to be continuously there to help. Perhaps as important as the first two reasons put together is the fact that in the back-home situation people have tasks to fulfill and face the pressures typical of a crisis-oriented, competitive organization.

To put this another way, since people live in a pattern A world, a quasi or actual laboratory experience will tend to be valued (by those who wish to increase their competence) because it sanctions such behavior as openness and trust.

However, if the individuals did not learn the interpersonal behavior of the pattern B world, then the laboratory may be experienced as highly involving but not very applicable to the back-home situation. If so, then one would predict fewer demands for the OD people because their value would be seen as limited to off-the-job settings.

5. Problems of evaluation

These findings raise some questions about the speed of change, its effectiveness during a short time period, and, therefore, the way one evaluated the effectiveness of the OD program.

Given the vacillating, nonlinear movement of change, it becomes very difficult to measure its effectiveness accurately. The results would be very different if the measurements were taken when the organization was at its peak of progress or had temporarily regressed. Also, what if half the client system was progressing and the other half was not? Could division within the client system have created measures that cancelled each other out? Also, may not a criterion for success be no change, over time, on such scores as mistrust, conformity, etc., because as has been suggested, the natural trend is toward organizational entropy?

One might, therefore, question the advisability of time series measures without also identifying the process of transition. If the pain, ambiguity, frustration, etc., were not there, either the client system would be very unusual or the changes might not be particularly deep and long lasting.

The writer has emphasized the position that change may be considered when it has been so well integrated within the organization that the original problems do not reoccur and that progress is continued. In client systems B and C it became evident that one of the biggest barriers toward integrated or internalized change was the inability of the top executives to give valid information without creating defensiveness, to receive information accurately, to create groups that were effective in operation and task achievement. This would at least raise a question in our minds of the permanency of change in a system where the individuals have not increased their interpersonal skills or the effectiveness of their groups.

For example, Schmuck, Runkel, and Langmeyer (1969); Beckhard (1969); and Blake and Mouton (1969) have presented evidence of organizational changes in the client systems with which they have worked without heavy focus on developing competence in such factors as minimally evaluative, minimally attributive, minimally controlling feedback, etc. If the clients did not develop such skills, then how did the changes come about? Could it be, as it was in the case of organization C, that clients used the very definition of a situation as a development experience, and the simple presence of the interventionist they evaluated as competent unfroze them to be more open, to be more experimental, to be less attributive (because they can see the interventionist behaving in these ways or because the interventionist helps them to communicate more effectively)? Is it possible that the changes will not fade out, but more complex changes will not tend to be designed and executed without the persuasion and competence of the interventionist?

The most important learning that may come from our study is how long, painful, confusing, difficult, and frustrating the transition period is going to be for those who choose to develop a YB world. Moving from XA to YB will place them in contact with and require them to confront some of our deepest values and concepts about the nature of man, his worth, and his position in the scheme of organizational life.

These questions have not been raised until recently, because our society has been occupied with solving what Maslow has called the "basic problems of fulfilling the physiological and security needs." The major criterion in developing organizations has been efficient production of goods or services. We have succeeded rather well in this phase of our existence. Our society, therefore, has come to be populated and dominated by organizations that can produce and can compete effectively throughout the world. As a result, the people enjoy the highest degree of fulfillment of the physiological and security needs known to man.

But, as Maslow predicted, the very success will lead to a new challenge. The people will begin to think increasingly about and seek intensively for new dimensions of personal growth and self-actualization. As these needs become dominant, the frustrations will increase because all the traditional organizations of all our institutions are designed to be effective if most of the participants gain minimal self-actualization (the exceptions are the managers and elite experts).

The frustration will not be silenced in the name of keeping a good thing going and not rocking the boat. People will feel them even more intensively and, because of their increasing sense of self-worth, may begin to resent the organizations and their establishment elite. As a result of the frustration and anger, they may look for ways to be critical. They may focus on their ineffectiveness and dry rot, which would not be too difficult to find. Unless concrete steps are taken to redesign our organizations and their managements, there is the possibility that people will not wait; and in their frustration they may destroy the very systems that have given and could continue to give them so much.

To redesign organizations and institutions requires the most searching inquiry into the nature of order, control, and organization as well as innovation and growth. Research will also be needed to provide the engineering know-how that will help us leave where we are and travel to where we want to be.

And this leads to another terribly difficult challenge. Research has its own technocracy. It utilizes processes of free inquiry that leave the subject about as free as the man on the assembly line. As the writer has suggested, traditional, rigorous research methods tend to create human systems of the XA variety (Argyris, 1968). To compound the felony the established way of using the knowledge, once it is produced, is to give it to planners and systems (public and private) that are already in power. Thus, the knowledge is not only produced in an XA world, it is disseminated and implemented in an XA fashion. What may prevent this felony from becoming intolerable is that little knowledge has been generated. Therefore there is little to give to the planners and to the institutions that, in effect, would increase their power.

But, as we have pointed out continuously in this book, the very dearth of knowledge may be a blessing in disguise. We may have time to work our way out of the bind. First, research technocracy can be designed which will involve the subjects as genuine participants. They can be brought into the problem-solving process early and in such a way that the resultant findings are relevant for them (Argyris, 1970).

To bring the researcher, planner, and citizen together requires a relationship where they trust each other and find that they may gain from each other. Such possibilities are inherent in a YB world. So we find our end and our means are the same, that valid and useful knowledge about a YB world requires continual research and cooperation in ways that explore and experiment with YB variables.

This line of reasoning leads one to question the idea that research can be separated from action. Research is needed to study the action; neither the research nor the action will be seen as worthwhile unless they can be connected to the new human requirements that people must have if the quality of their life is to be raised. Similarly the accomplishment of tasks or the production of anything cannot be separated from the health and development of the organization seeking to accomplish the tasks. The latter helps to guarantee not only production but also continued existence; the former buys the economic and social resources that will be needed to help us design and operate healthy organizations that value and require human actualization.

These findings also confirm the generalization that participation per se may not be the basic goal toward which to strive. Bringing people together or giving them influence over decisions does not guarantee the effectiveness of their problem solving, the quality of their decision, and the strength of their commitment to the decision. From our research, we would state the following preliminary generalizations:

1. People in our society, through their acculturation and education, are programmed to behave according to the pyramidal values (Chapter 1). This means that if people are brought together to participate, they will tend to create ineffective relationships and group dynamics; they will tend to be blind about their contribution, but aware of the contributions of others to the ineffectiveness; but they

will not tend to express the latter views openly, and if they do, they will tend to do so in a manner that causes more difficulties.

2. Participation can become effective if human beings are helped to develop the skills and the self-acceptance and confidence required.[8] This is not an easy task. As we have seen from organization A, neither good intentions nor education of some of the members of the group guarantees the skills or the increase in confidence. An increase in interpersonal competence by a few may threaten the others (organization B); nor does the education of the entire top-management group guarantee success. They are still faced with transferring their learning to the back-home situation, and they still need maps and guideposts regarding new organizational structures and managerial controls (organization C).

3. Learning the skills of interpersonal competence is not simple. The reader is encouraged to experiment with trying to get a task accomplished (let us say in a group) and do so by speaking in observed categories, with minimal evaluation, minimal attribution, and minimal inconsistency. Our subjects found that for several years they had difficulty with this requirement. To be sure, we have argued that the original courses and the OD specialists did not help as much as they could. This argument suggests an important way in which education can be redesigned. It also reemphasizes the difficulty inherent in the type of learning being suggested, since the experts (OD specialists)

---

[8] Some may suggest that participation can be effective under firm but fair control, such as Robert's rules. In our experience such rules do bring about order and control. However, they rarely encourage openness, trust, risk taking, and a genuine working through of issues.

have difficulty in behaving according to the new values and skills.

Why is it so difficult to learn to behave more competently with other human being and groups? First, because the concept of interpersonal competence presently accepted and taught is deeply engrained in us, is strongly supported by society, and is one key to organizational success. It is not stretching the point too much to say that people tend to succeed in the organizational world *if* they show an acceptable degree of interpersonal incompetence and an equivalent blindness to this incompetence, supported by minimal guilt and a first-rate mind to accomplish the technical tasks or objectives.

Second, individuals, as we have seen, find the reeducative process frustrating and embarrassing. They have great difficulty in accepting their interpersonal incompetence, especially since they have been rewarded because of it, and since the behavior that is labeled as competent has yet to be "proven" or accepted by our society.

They are also embarrassed to realize that they have to learn a completely new language. They are bewildered when they see that the language cannot be learned in a mechanistic and rote form. Unless the new language mirrors what they genuinely feel inside, its nonauthenticity is easily identified, and the individual is seen by others, and he soon sees himself, as incongruent or hypocritical. The language of trust can only be authentic with an individual who is capable of trusting; the same is true for openness, concern, experimenting. Yet, these are the very behaviors we have shown are rarely manifested in life.

One way of describing the difficulty is to picture what happens to an individual when he is problem solving. Simon (1969) has shown that the individual searches to identify the problems. Then he looks into his stored-up information for guidance as to how he should act. In this case he is soon confronted with two startling discoveries. Most of the stored-up information is either worthless or harmful. For the first time since childhood he may feel a genuine sense of loss and helplessness, feelings which he has not experienced, especially if he has been successful.

He must now seek inwardly to find strength to deal with helplessness and failure. He must also seek outwardly to connect with other human beings in a way that neither he nor they have tried before. Simultaneously, they all will have to strive to create new group norms, new mores, indeed a new culture that will sanction and protect the new behavior.

Thus learning the language of authentic relationships is much more than a mechanistic learning experience. It means a reexamination of oneself, one's contribution to human relationship, the culture in which one lives, and the values to which one is committed.

The challenges of organizational development

One of the basic dilemmas of organizational development is that OD activities, if they are to be effective, require that they be organically grafted upon the existing system. But to generate an organic graft, it must not violate the present internal makeup of the system. If the graft does not violate the present makeup of the system, then it will not be particularly new. However, the objectives of OD activities in A, B, and C were designed to lead to systems that were significantly different and, therefore, would strongly violate the present defenses of these systems.

Some interventionists prefer to play down the basic differences in values and behavior between XA and YB hoping that, as time goes by, they will vanish slowly. The difficulty with this strategy may be made explicit if we examine two implicit assumptions inherent in it. The first implicit assumption is that, given the present state of client systems, it is predictable that they would reject OD activities that were oriented toward YB. However as they came to understand these OD activities, they would no longer resist them. The problem is that the interventionist begins his relationship with the client by violating his own values about hiding or manipulating information. Unfortunately, this apparently innocent violation that the interventionist believes he can easily manage "as things progress" frequently becomes the basis for a credibility gap which can lead to extreme difficulties and failure (Argyris, 1970).

The second implicit assumption of this type of intervention is that the interventionist may not trust himself to be authoritative without being authoritarian, to cope with the client anxiety early in the relationship, and to be willing to accept genuine resistance and, if necessary, rejection of the OD design. Thus the strategy may be unrealizingly developed to protect the interventionist from his anxieties.

Turning to management, their most frequent way of coping with the differences between their present values and behavior and those implicit in OD activities is to conceive of the latter as something to be developed, as an addition to, not a reorganization of, the present system. For example, in all three organizations top managements' interest in OD began primarily from a dissatisfaction about past organizational performance and leadership style or an awareness (usually from comments made by subordinates) of a lack of rational planning regarding the human resources.

The reaction of the top management in A was typical. Given the diagnosis that something was missing, and given it should be consonant with the present system, then the action step was "find a new program, plug it in, and control it." The implicit assumption was that the present executive system did not have to be reexamined, but that a new program be grafted on to its "side." Imagine if the interventionist had attended the meeting and had given the charismatic talk asked for by the top management. He would have included some blunt talk about how management must change if individuals are to be developed. Assume further that the bluntness was presented without anger and punishment and carefully served with several funny but telling stories which won over the management. The session would end with an "acceptance" by the top management of the objectives, symbolized, probably, by a charismatic closing talk by the president. The interventionist would never have become aware that the top management's enthusiastic acceptance might be partially a defense to hide their anxieties. The reader may recall that the top executives of company A who talked openly and convincingly about human development, who interacted with the interventionist to explore some of their behavior, and who decided to go ahead with the interventionist's suggested design were (during the final meeting) willing to go along with the policy that management by objectives was great for everyone but them.

This basic dilemma of OD, to be fully integrated with the system, yet help to transform it, if not faced openly, can become the basis for diplomatic, if not phony, programs. However it can become the foundation for progress if the clients are helped to see that the dilemma is their challenge, their opportunity to come face to face with their personal and organizational responsibility.

This is not an easy task to accomplish. Most executives (indeed it may be argued that most individuals) are culturally programmed to behave in ways that inhibit OD and to be systematically blind to their inhibitory behavior (Argyris, 1969 and 1970). In these three organizations, for example, we found that the natural behavior of the three executive groups before reeducation (and in some cases after reeducation) was to minimize, in their relationships with each other and with subordinates, such key behavior as the expression of feelings, helping others to own up to their ideas and to be open, experimenting and risk taking, and establishing norms of individuality and trust. Moreover in cases A and B (with the exception of the top subgroup in the latter) the natural reaction of the executives was to be blind to the discrepancy between the requirements of an effective OD program and the requirements created by their behavior in their everyday interactions in managing their organizations.

Again difficulties will arise if the interventionist accepts this state of affairs, develops a program (such as management by objectives), plugs it in, and hopes that the executives will alter their behavior as they participate in the program. There are no built-in mechanisms for ineffective relationships to change by themselves and become effective ones when the executives at all levels tend to be blind to their ineffectiveness; when the norms about effective leadership are not subject to questioning; and when the subordinates are, therefore, careful not to feed back information to the superior about the incongruency between his behavior and his words.

To make matters more difficult is the genuine disbelief

that many executives manifest when it is suggested to them that it will not be easy to change their behavior, even if they wanted to change it. These executives, who have become successful by "getting a hold of any problem and solving it," who have many experiences of making successful self-fulfilling prophecies about the behavior of their system, are now befuddled by the assertion that they cannot use the same logic to change their own behavior. They have faith in rational education that is charismatically presented; "You tell us what to do and we will do it."

The evidence, however, is to the contrary. Men cannot implant a new way of behaving by willing it. To will it is a necessary but not a sufficient step. They must unfreeze their old and learn new behavior and attitudes. Indeed, a genuine test of whether executives want to change is if they are willing to go beyond the necessary and work on the sufficient. Thus, I would say that the willingness of the top management in organization A to explore the creation of OD activities was probably based on their readiness to make primarily skin-surface changes in their behavior and not ones that would occur if their present values, attitudes, and defenses about effective human relationships were genuinely unfrozen and altered.

To make matters even more difficult, being willing to work hard for genuine change is not sufficient. Internal commitment to the change processes is necessary. In organization B, we saw what happened when some "willing" executives were confronted by a process that required that they genuinely choose to alter their values, attitudes, and behavior. An entire spectrum of fears and prejudices became evident ranging from "soft management" to the danger of creating "a runaway locomotive." These fears, in turn, were tied to deeper defenses, probably learned early in life, regarding how to deal with one's own feelings of aggression; how to prevent rejection by oneself of others and they of him; how to control others in such a way that maintaining the relationship did not require changes in one's own defense makeup. These do not change overnight.

Does this mean that changes cannot occur without deeper psychotherapy? There are some, like Zalesnik, who suggest that changes of the kind that we are discussing are so deep that only psychotherapy can be effective (Zalesnik, 1965). Zalesnik's hypothesis may be correct, but it is still an hypothesis to be tested. Recent thinking suggests that each level of change is valid under different conditions (Argyris, 1970; Harrison, 1970). Let us imagine it were possible to measure accurately the degree of openness people have toward the processes of unfreezing and learning new values and behavior. We may also imagine that it would be possible to find that some groups and individuals are more open than others (Argyris, 1968). The more the individuals and groups are closed, the more they may be conceived of as internally conflicted and the stronger are their defenses against change. Moreover, the more difficult it will be for them to learn under the OD conditions suggested in this book; for example, the more difficult it will be for individuals to give or to hear accurately valid information that is given in observed categories, that is minimally evaluative and attributive, and that creates double binds.

The less the individuals or groups are able to learn under OD conditions, the less they will be able to learn from their peers. Under these conditions, OD activities may not be the most effective ones to suggest. More appropriate may be that the individuals consider some form of group psychotherapy so that they can be helped by an expert to become unconflicted enough so that they can learn from peers. After they have overcome these problems, then organizational development activities may become relevant.

Zalesnik argues that, ". . . institutions may change only with increased control man achieves over his instinctual strivings. . . ." I see no difficulty with this statement. The difficulty comes, I believe, because some are willing to hypothesize that psychotherapy is not the only way for an individual to increase his control over his instinctual strivings. It is possible, some of us hypothesize, for control to be acquired through gaining interpersonal competence *and* living in systems of human relationships which encourage and support continual self-growth and self-control.

The quantitative scores of the executives in organization C shows that their behavior can be altered in the direction of greater competence. The data also showed that increases in individual competence did not necessarily transfer to the back-home situation if the primary group and the organizational structure, controls, and policies did not support such changes. The data in B and C also showed that the behavioral changes are viable enough that they can be reactivated when they become acceptable, and that the changes are not erased even under extreme pressure to do so (as in case B).

Zalesnik criticizes organizational development activities for underplaying, ". . . the role of leadership in organization and societies as a significant factor toward change. There can be little institutional development apart from educated and wise leadership" (Zalesnik, 1965, p. 611). Again there is no argument with the statement. Anyone who has ever been in an effective T-group or reads this and other books on OD knows that leadership and power are key issues and that organizational change without wise leadership is not going to be successful. The issue, I believe, revolves around what is wise leadership and who has it. Unfortunately Zalesnik does not define it, and, as such, may unintentionally make himself an ideologist, a role that he rejects as being unhelpful and attributes to many who work with OD activities.

Psychotherapy, especially psychoanalysis, has traditionally assumed that the wise leadership resides primarily with the therapist. The OD activities, on the other hand, do assume that leadership can be spread around, depending upon people's skills and competences. We do assume that human beings can help each other more than psychoanalysts would. Indeed, Zalesnik does not discuss the literature (of which two recent reviews are Gendlin and Pychlak, 1970; and Shapiro, 1969) that questions the centrality of the role of the therapist as conceptualized in his terms. It may be that effective therapists are those who know how to give genuine warmth and support and are able to help others do the same (Truax et al., 1968). Thus, when one states that institutions may change only through wise leadership, one needs to be careful to make clear that he is not imposing the requirement a particular group of therapists hold if they are to be effective.

Finally, the experience in organization C suggests that willingness and internal commitment may not be sufficient for effective OD. An executive group requires continual help, especially in three critical areas. They are (1) giving and receiving valid information; (2) creating effective group behavior and norms; and (3) designing new kinds of organizational structures, managerial controls, and reward systems that reinforce the new behavior so that the managerial behavior, the organizational structure, etc., become congruent with the OD philosophy.

Although all these requirements are important, the experiences described in this book suggest that OD activities are begun with making the executive behavior congruent with the OD philosophy. The objective of congruence means that the executives make a personal and active choice about OD. The executives' internal commitment is necessary because, as we have seen in organizations B and C, the transition period is a very long one and full of ambiguities and tensions. If the executives are not internally committed, they may easily regress and retreat from their stipulated goals. Such a retreat tends to be precisely what the disbelieving subordinates predict and the second-rate ones hope for. The retreat "confirms" that OD is simply a gimmick and that under stress the top executives regress to their old and (in the eyes of the subordinates) genuine style. This means that the second-rate executives can relax because they can continue to use the defensiveness of the system as a barricade behind which to hide their incompetence. It is the first-rate men who will get discouraged and probably leave or slowly become acculturated to the system.

The transition period of going from a more mechanistic closed-to-learning system to a more organic open-to-learning system is much longer and more painful than has been realized. Part of the pain will be reduced and the length shortened as research and experience suggest how organizational development can be brought about more effectively. However, the experience of the pain and the expense of time may always need to be there as an impetus and a price for growth, helping to guarantee (especially to those with less power) that new ideas from social science cannot be used indiscriminately to manipulate people into worlds that are described as new, but in reality are the old clothed in different words and actions.

The challenge of organizational development is close to, if not part of, the very foundations for the design of a new quality of life that looks upon man's potentiality as not only something to be revered in words but also to be continually actualized in systems that respect and require human dignity and organizational health.

Bibliography

Adelson, J.: "Personality," *Annual Review of Psychology,* 20: 218, 1969.

Argyris, Chris: "Management Information Systems: The Challenge to Rationality and Emotionality," *Management Science,* (17) 6: B-275-292, 1971.

—— : *Intervention Theory and Method: a Behavioral Science View,* Addison-Wesley Publishing Company, Reading, Mass., 1970.

—— : "The Incompleteness of Social Psychological Theory," *American Psychologist* (24) 10: 893-908, 1969.

—— : "On the Effectiveness of Research and Development Organizations," *American Scientist* (56) 4: 344-355, 1968.

—— : "Interpersonal Barriers to Decision Making," *Harvard Business Review* (22) 2: 84-97, 1966.

—— : "The Integration of the Individual and the Organization," in George B. Strother (ed.), *Social Science Approaches to Business Behavior,* The Dorsey Press and Richard D. Irwin, Inc., Homewood, Ill., 1962, pp. 57-98.

—— : *Interpersonal Competence and Organizational Effective-*

ness, The Dorsey Press and Richard D. Irwin, Inc., Homewood, Ill., 1962.

———: *Personality and Organization,* Harper & Brothers, New York, 1957.

———: *Integrating the Individual and the Organization,* John Wiley & Sons, Inc., New York, 1954.

Beckhard, Richard: *Organization Development: Strategies and Models,* Addison-Wesley Publishing Company, Reading, Mass., 1969.

Bennis, Warren G.: *Organizational Development: Its Nature, Origin and Prospects,* Addison-Wesley Publishing Company, Inc., Reading, Mass., 1969.

———: "Leadership Theory and Administrative Behavior," *Administrative Science Quarterly* (4) 3: 259–301, 1959.

Berlew, D. E., and D. T. Hall: "The Socialization of Managers: Effects of Expectations on Performance," *Administrative Science Quarterly,* 11: 207–224, 1966.

Blake, Robert R., and Jane S. Mouton: *Building a Dynamic Corporation through Grid Organization Development,* Addison-Wesley Publishing Company, Inc., Reading, Mass., 1969.

Blau, P. M., and W. R. Scott: *Formal Organizations,* Chandler Publishing Company, San Francisco, 1962.

Blumberg, P.: *Industrial Democracy: The Sociology of Participation,* Schacken Books, New York, 1960.

Burns, Tom, and G. M. Stalker: *The Management of Innovation,* Tavistock Publications, London, 1961, pp. 120–121.

Campbell, Donald T.: "Considering the Case against Experimental Evaluation of Social Innovation," *Administrative Science Quarterly* (15) 1: 110–113, 1970.

Cronbach, L. J., and G. C. Gleser: *Psychological Tests and Personnel Decisions,* The University of Illinois Press, Urbana, 1965, pp. 144–148.

Dubin, Robert: "Industrial Workers' World: A Study of the 'Central Life Interests' of Industrial Workers," in E. Smigel (ed.), *Work and Leisure,* Yale University Press, New Haven, Conn., 1963, pp. 53–72.

Dunnette, Marvin D., Richard D. Arvey, and Paul Banas: "Why Do They Leave," Department of Psychology, University of Minnesota, Minneapolis, 1970 (mimeographed).

Fiedler, Fred E.: *A Theory of Leadership Effectiveness,* McGraw-Hill Book Company, New York, 1967.

Fleishman, E. A.: "Leadership Climate, Human Relations, and Supervisory Behavior," in E. A. Fleishman (ed.), *Studies in Personnel and Industrial Psychology,* The Dorsey Press and Richard D. Irwin, Inc., Homewood, Ill., 1961.

Ford, Robert N.: *Motivation through the Work Itself,* American Management Association, Inc., New York, 1969.

Gardner, John: "America in the Twenty-third Century," *New York Times,* editorial, July 27, 1968.

Geertz, C.: "The Impact of the Concept of Culture," in J. R. Platt (ed.), *New Views of the Nature of Man,* The University of Chicago Press, Chicago, 1965, pp. 105–107.

Gendlin, Eugene T., and J. R. Pychlak: "Psychotherapeutic Processes," *Annual Review of Psychology,* 21:155–190, 1970.

Goldthorpe, J., D. Lockwood, F. Beckhofer, and J. Platt: *The Affluent Worker: Industrial Attitudes and Behavior,* Cambridge University Press, London, 1968.

Greiner, L. E.: "Patterns of Organization Change," *Harvard Business Review,* (45) 3: 119–123, 1967.

Haire, M., E. E. Ghiselli, and Lyman Porter: "Cultural Patterns in the Role of the Manager," *Industrial Relations,* 2: 95–117, 1963.

Harrison, R.: "Choosing the Depth of Organizational Intervention," *Journal of Applied Behavioral Science,* (6) 2: 181–202, 1970.

Hoopes, T.: *The Limits of Intervention,* David McKay Company, Inc., New York, 1969.

Kahn, Robert L., Donald M. Wolfe, Robert P. Quinn, J. Diedrick Snoek, and Robert A. Rosenthal: *Organizational Stress: Studies in Role Conflict and Ambiguity,* John Wiley & Sons, Inc., New York, 1964.

Lawrence, P., and J. W. Lorsch: "Organizations and Environment Managing Differentiation and Integration," Harvard Graduate School of Business Administration, Cambridge, Mass., 1967.

Lawshe, G. H.: "What Can Industrial Psychology Do for Small Business? (A Symposium): Employee Selection," *Personnel Psychology,* 5: 31–34, 1952.

Lewin, K.: *Field Theory in Social Science,* Dorwin Cartwright (ed.), Harper & Brothers, New York, 1951.

Likert, Rensis: *The Human Organization,* McGraw-Hill Book Company, New York, 1967.

————: *New Patterns of Management,* McGraw-Hill Book Company, New York, 1961.

Litwak, E.: "Models of Bureaucracy Which Permit Conflict," *American Journal of Sociology,* (67) 2: 177–184, 1961.

McGregor, D.: *The Professional Manager,* McGraw-Hill Book Company, New York, 1967.

————: *The Human Side of Enterprise,* McGraw-Hill Book Company, New York, 1960.

———: "Conditions of Effective Leadership in Industrial Organizations," *Journal of Consulting Psychology*, 8: 56–83, 1944.

Marrow, A. J., David G. Bowers, and S. E. Seashore: *Management by Participation*, Harper & Row, Publishers, Incorporated, New York, 1967.

Maslow, Abraham: *Motivation and Personality*, Harper & Brothers, New York, 1954.

Maurer, J. G.: "Work Role Involvement of Industrial Supervisors," Bureau of Business and Economic Research, Graduate School of Business, Michigan State University Press, East Lansing, 1969.

Mayo, Elton: *Human Problems of an Industrial Civilization*, The Macmillan Company, New York, 1933.

Meyer, H. H., E. Kay, and J. R. P. French: "Split Roles in Performance Appraisal," *Harvard Business Review*, 43: 123–129, 1965.

New York Times, March 27, 1970, pp. 1, 4.

Oshry, B. I., and R. Harrison: "Transfer From Here-and-Now to There-and-Then: Changes in Organizational Problem Diagnosis Stemming From T-Group Training," *Journal of Applied Behavioral Science*, (2) 2: 185–198, 1966.

Pettigrew, R. F.: "Personality and Sociocultural Factors in Intergroup Attitudes: A Cross-National Comparison," *Journal of Conflict Resolution*, 2: 29–42, 1958.

Roethlisberger, F. J., and W. J. Dickson: *Management and the Worker*, Harvard University Press, Cambridge, Mass., 1949.

Sarason, Seymour B.: "The Creation of Settings," in Robert B. Kugel and Wolf Wolfensberger (eds.), *Changing Patterns in Residential Services for the Mentally Retarded*, President's Committee on Mental Retardation, Washington, D.C., January 10, 1969.

Schein, E. H.: *Organizational Psychology*, Prentice-Hall, Inc., Englewood Cliffs, N. J., 1965.

———: "How to Break in the College Graduate," *Harvard Business Review* (42) 6: 68–76, 1964.

Schmuck, Richard A., Philip J. Runkel, and Daniel Langmeyer: "Improving Organizational Problem Solving in a School Faculty," *Journal of Applied Behavioral Science* (5) 4: 455–483, 1969.

Shapiro, D. A.: "Empathy, Warmth and Genuineness in Psychotherapy," *British Journal of Social and Clinical Psychology*, 8: 350–361, 1969.

Simon, Herbert: *The Science of the Artificial*, The MIT Press, Cambridge, Mass., 1969.

Sorcher, Melvin: "The Effects of Employee Involvement on Work Performance," *Personnel Research Planning and Practices*, General Electric Company, New York, 1969.

Strauss, George: "Some Notes on Power-Equalization," in H. J. Leavitt (ed.), *The Social Sciences of Organizations: Four Perspectives*, Prentice-Hall, Inc., Englewood Cliffs, N.J., 1963.

Tannenbaum, A. S.: *Control in Organizations*, McGraw-Hill Book Company, New York, 1968.

Trist, Eric, et al.: *Organizational Choice*, Tavistock Institute, London, 1962.

Truax, C. B., D. G. Wargo, J. D. Frank, S. D. Imber, C. C. Battle, R. Hoehn-Saree, E. H. Nash, and A. R. Stone: "Therapist Empathy, Genuineness and Warmth and Patient Therapeutic Outcome," *Journal of Clinical Psychology*, 22: 331–334, 1966.

Weiss, R. S., and M. Rein: "The Evaluation of Broad-aim Programs: Experimental Design, Its Difficulties, and an Alternative," *Administrative Science Quarterly* (15) 1: 97–109, 1970.

Wohlking, Wallace: "Attitude Change, Behavior Change; the Role of the Training Department," 19th Annual Training Institute, New York State School of Industrial and Labor Relations, Cornell University, Ithaca, New York, 1969 (mimeographed).

Whyte, W. F.: *Men At Work*, The Dorsey Press and Richard D. Irwin, Inc., Homewood, Ill., 1961.

Zalesnik, A.: "Interpersonal Relations in Organizations," in James G. March (ed.), *Handbook of Organizations*, Rand McNally & Company, Chicago, 1965, pp. 574–613.

Zuponov, J., and A. S. Tannenbaum: "The Distribution of Control in Some Yugoslav Industrial Organizations as Perceived by Members," in Arnold S. Tannenbaum (ed.), *Control in Organizations*, McGraw-Hill Book Company, New York, pp. 73–89, 1968.

Name Index

Name Index

Subject Index

Subject Index